Insight Compact Guide: St Lucia

Written by: Lesley Gordon
Updated by: Sarah Cameron
Edited by: Catherine Dreghorn

Photography by: Richard Nowitz, with additional photography by ATV Paradise Tours 105; Banana Cake/Alamy 70/1; Anthony Blake 60; Corbis 80/2, 91; Ian Cumming/Axiom 75/2; Jerry Dennis/Apa 88; Fotolia 53/2, 80/1; Lesley Gordon 65/2, 66; iStock 5BL, 9, 45/2, 57/1, 73/1,2; Bob Krist 6, 8/1, 8/2, 10/2, 13, 15, 16, 20–1, 47, 48/2, 52, 54/2, 62/2, 69/2, 71, 74, 81, 83, 84, 85/2, 85/3; Nature 17; Bert Nienhuis 89/2; Rain Forest Adventures 4CL; Rex Features 89/1; Rex Resorts 37/1, 2; courtesy of the St Lucia Tourist Board 61, 62/2; Smugglers Cove Resort & Spa 116; Terraqua 17/1, 50–1, 67; Topham 14, 82/1, 93; courtesy of the Balenbouche Estate 119; courtesy of Llewellyn Xavier 44, 88
Cover picture by: 4Corners Images, *back cover pictures:* fotolia
Picture Editor: Tom Smyth
Design: Tanvir Virdee
Maps: Apa Cartography Department

Series Editor: Sarah Sweeney
Publishing Manager: Rachel Fox

CONTACTING THE EDITORS: As every effort is made to provide accurate information in this publication, we would appreciate it if readers would call our attention to any errors and omissions by contacting:
Apa Publications, PO Box 7910, London SE1 1WE, England.
Email: insight@apaguide.co.uk

Information has been obtained from sources believed to be reliable, but its accuracy and completeness, and the opinions based thereon, are not guaranteed.

© 2011 APA Publications (UK) Ltd.

First Edition 2004
Second Edition 2011

Printed in China by CTPS

Distributed in the UK & Ireland by:
GeoCenter International Ltd
Meridian House, Churchill Way West, Basingstoke,
Hampshire RG21 6YR
sales@geocenter.co.uk

Worldwide distribution enquiries:
APA Publications GmbH & Co. Verlag KG (Singapore Branch)
7030 Ang Mo Kio Ave 5, 08-65 Northstar @ AMK, Singapore 569880
apasin@singnet.com.sg

w w w . i n s i g h t g u i d e s . c o m

Introduction

Places

Culture

Travel Tips

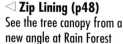

△ **Fond Doux Estate (p72)**
Cocoa pod at Fond Deux, a working plantation. Estate trails lead past ruined, 18th-century military buildings.

△ **Anse Chastanet (p67)**
An ideal spot for divers and snorkellers, with a resort and a marine reserve just metres from the beach.

◁ **Zip Lining (p48)**
See the tree canopy from a new angle at Rain Forest Adventures in Chassin.

△ **Balenbouche Estate (p77)** The plantation has an 18th-century water wheel and a mill once used to process sugar cane.

◁ **Pigeon Island (p40)**
A strategic military post used by British troops in the 18th century and the US armed forces in the 20th century.

△ **Diamond Falls (p68)**
The beautiful cascades are mineral rich; its waters are believed to be an effective treatment for rheumatism.

△ **Castries (p22)**
The city's colonial architecture has balconies adorned with gingerbread fretwork.

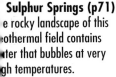

Sulphur Springs (p71)
e rocky landscape of this
othermal field contains
ter that bubbles at very
gh temperatures.

△ **The Pitons (p75)**
These volcanic cones are spectacular landmarks that feature on everything from T-shirts to tablecloths.

▷ **Grande Anse (p50)**
The endangered leatherback turtle hatchlings rush to the sea from protected nesting sites on the East Coast.

The Land of the Iguana

Every year, several hundred thousand people visit the tiny island of St Lucia (pronounced *Loo-sha*) which was known as Hewanorra (Land of the Iguana) to the early Amerindians. Visitors come for the archetypal Caribbean holiday of sand, sun and sea, but soon discover a wealth of other attractions and activities to enjoy.

Most of the year the weather is warm and sunny, tempered by trade winds and light showers. The Caribbean coast has long stretches of fine sand and healthy coral reefs, while the Atlantic-buffeted side provides good windsurfing and has nature reserves populated by rare wildlife. At the island's heart the rich land is lush with trees, and there are forest reserves in the mountains and on the Pitons, the landmark twin, cone-shaped peaks. In the valley below farmland punctuates the landscape.

There is also a colourful Creole culture and the people are, for the most part, open and friendly with a sense of fun and real pride in their homeland. Their bright and cheerful outlook on life is reflected in their cottage gardens, where flowers and vivid yellow-, red- and purple-leaved shrubs jostle for space with fruit trees and herbs.

For more than two centuries the land was the subject of bloody battles and a virtual tug-of-war ensued between the acquisitive French and British imperial powers who fought for control. Today, St Lucians still guard their island jealously, and rightly so, because with careful development the environment of this tropical paradise will remain a naturalist's dream.

POSITION AND LANDSCAPE

Lying at the southern end of the Lesser Antilles chain, St Lucia is about 2,100km (1,300 miles) from Florida, with Martinique 34km (21 miles) to the north, St Vincent to the south and Barbados 160km (100 miles) to the southeast. The island comprises 617 sq km (238 sq miles) of undulating hills and mountains covered with native trees,

Windward bound
The Windward Islands are made up of Dominica, St Lucia, St Vincent and the Grenadines, and Grenada.

Opposite: the spectacular Diamond Falls
Below: strolling along a beach on the island's north coast

Above: the St Lucia parrot (Amazona versicolor) is known locally as jacquot

The Tree of Life

The coconut palm is known as the 'tree of life' because every part of the tree can be put to good use. The palm leaf is used for roofing, basket-weaving and making hats; the trunk is used in construction, and the brown outer fibre and husk of the nut is used in mattresses and pillows. Coconut water, drunk directly from the nut, makes a refreshing drink, while the mature nut is tasty as a snack or in cooking. Coconut oil is also used in toiletries.

coconut palms, banana plantations and several types of forest, home to a variety of wildlife such as lizards, hermit crabs and the national bird, the St Lucia green parrot *(Amazona versicolor)*.

The second-largest of the Windward Islands group – only Dominica is bigger – volcanic St Lucia is 43km (27 miles) long and 22km (14 miles) wide, with beaches of black or golden sand, hot sulphur springs, a scenic mountain range and rich, fertile soil. The twin peaks, Gros Piton and Petit Piton, are smaller than the island's highest point, Morne Gimie (950m/3,118ft).

The centre of the island is dominated by a mountainous landscape carpeted with lush vegetation. More than 300m (1,000ft) above sea level, the cool rainforest covers a large part of the island's interior and southern areas, with a series of stunning waterfalls. Soufrière volcano is dormant – there has been no volcanic activity on the island since 1766 – but vents hydrogen sulphide gases and steam. A tell-tale odour, rather like rotten eggs, pervades the island's sulphur springs in the Soufrière area, where the rocky landscape is dotted with craters blackened with iron sulphate and pools of bubbling water that reach temperatures of 170°C (338°F). Visitors exploring the Edmund Forest Reserve on foot can take a dip in the breathtaking En Bas Saut waterfall in the south, or sneak away to smaller, lesser-known falls. Wildlife lovers head to the Maria Islands, an offshore sanctuary where an endemic lizard sports the national colours, but access is barred during the nesting season for hundreds of seabirds.

MARINE LIFE

Lashed by the Atlantic Ocean and bathed by the Caribbean Sea, St Lucia has varied marine life, with protected coral reefs and colourful inhabitants such as angel and parrot fish. It is one of the world's top snorkelling and scuba diving destinations, bringing people back time and again. Whale- and dolphin-watching off the coast can be fun, as can a day spent sport fishing, sailing on a yacht or catamaran, or simply paddling in the warm water.

CLIMATE AND WHEN TO GO

St Lucia has a tropical, humid climate that provides warm sunshine most of the year, cooled by north-eastern trade winds. Showers during the rainy season keep the land lush and green. During the tourist high season (December to April) temperatures can reach 28–31°C (82–88°F) accompanied by a light breeze and short showers. The hottest months are June to August, with temperatures averaging 30°C (86°F), while December and January are the coolest, when night and early morning temperatures can drop to 21°C (69°F). The average daily temperature from November to February is 27°C (81°F) and about 22°C (72°F) at night. From April to October daytime temperatures of 23–29°C (73–84°F) are not uncommon. It is several degrees cooler in the rainforest and mountain villages, and colder still on the mountain peaks.

The rainy season runs from June to the end of November and is characterised by sporadic heavy showers. The annual rainfall can be up to three times higher in the mountains in the south (3,450mm/136 inches) than on the coast in the north (1,500mm/59 inches), which contributes to the lush forest vegetation and fertile farmland.

The hurricane season is generally between June and November, coinciding with the rainy season. Storms are the most damaging weather phenomenon in the Lesser Antilles, but St Lucia's

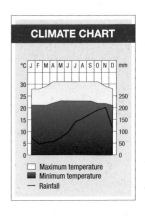

CLIMATE CHART

□ Maximum temperature
■ Minimum temperature
— Rainfall

Take a dolphin-watching trip to see pods of dolphins

marinas and sheltered harbours on the Leeward (Caribbean) coast are popular with the sailing fraternity. However, the hilly terrain means St Lucia is particularly susceptible to mudslides caused by torrential rain, which often lead to casualties and huge farming losses. In 2010, landslides caused by rain associated with Hurricane Tomas killed 14 people.

POPULATION

Below: water sports on Hummingbird Beach, Soufrière
Bottom: schoolchildren in Soufrière

The island population, which numbers about 174,000, is a pot pourri of people of African, Amerindian, European and East Indian descent. Around 67,000 live in the small area of the capital, Castries, and its environs. In fact, almost 50 percent of the entire population inhabits urban areas. There are more young people than old, which is not uncommon in a developing country, with almost a quarter of the population under 15 years old and fewer than 10 percent over 65.

Even if their ancestors were born here, it is safe to say that no one in St Lucia is truly indigenous. European settlement, indentured labour and slavery helped to determine the ethnic mix of the country. Disease, war and colonisation contributed to the disappearance of the island's Amerindian population, which was virtually wiped out by the time enslaved Africans were introduced in the late

17th-century. Few people can trace their ancestry directly to the early Amerindians, known as Kalinago, as they can in neighbouring Dominica. However, there are St Lucians who are of mixed African and Amerindian blood.

People with an African heritage are likely to be descendants of the slaves brought as forced labour to work the land, while St Lucians of European heritage are probably the descendants of settlers, plantation owners and poor white labourers. There are also communities of East Indians, descendants of indentured labourers who arrived after the abolition of slavery. Today, around 80 percent of the population is of African origin, under 3 percent of East Indian extraction, with 12 percent of mixed heritage, and people of European origin making up the remainder. This is a Creole society in its broadest sense: a rich and rare combination of races, cultures, languages and cuisine.

LANGUAGE AND CULTURE

Although St Lucia has been a British territory since 1814 and the official language is English, French culture pervades. A melodic French Creole (Kwéyòl) is spoken by more than 90 percent of people in informal arenas and, due to a drive to preserve and promote Creole traditions, is increasingly used in official circles as well. It has been suggested that a large percentage of children do not speak English until they go to school. Creole culture and heritage is important and efforts are being made to hold on to the rich folklore, music and language. There are annual festivals, which include traditional storytellers, folk singers and dancers and carnival masqueraders.

The French influence can be seen in place and family names and also in the island's closeness to the neighbouring French *département* of Martinique. There are common linguistic elements within St Lucian and Martinican Creole. However, St Lucian Kwéyòl isn't as close to the French language as one might imagine.

Kwéyòl began as an oral language that initially helped the French and groups from different parts

Weather warning
A hurricane warning is issued when storm winds reach at least 119km (74 miles) per hour and high water and storm surges are expected within 24 hours. Warnings should identify specific coastal areas that may be affected by the storm. If ordered to evacuate to a hurricane shelter, follow designated routes as quickly as possible and take only what you will need, such as extra blankets, clothing, medication and a torch.

The game of warri (also called monkala) was imported from Africa

of the African continent communicate effectively. It was derived from elements of French, a variety of African vocabulary and grammar, English and a little Spanish. St Lucian Kwéyòl did not have an official written form until the 20th century and today many people who are fluent Kwéyòl speakers are not literate in the language.

Kwéyòl continues to gain legitimacy through the work of community groups and increasing published literature. In 1998 Kwéyòl was officially recognised in the St Lucia House of Assembly and in 1999 the New Testament was published in Kwéyòl, a project that took 15 years to complete. Jones Mondesir compiled the first reference and this work was followed by that of Paul Crosbie, David Frank, Emanuel Leon and Peter Samuel, who produced a Kwéyòl dictionary for the Ministry of Education, published in 2001.

Colonial architecture on Brazil Street, Castries (below) and at Fond Doux (bottom)

RELIGION

As recently as the 1980s approximately 95 percent of islanders were Roman Catholic but that figure has dropped to just under 70 percent due to the rise of evangelical, Pentecostal and other church groups such as Seventh Day Adventists. Anglican membership has remained consistent at about 2 percent. The church plays an important part in the lives of ordinary people, and attending services is as popular in urban areas as in rural villages.

Living by traditional Christian values hasn't prevented St Lucians from retaining elements of the old West African belief system and folklore – *obeah*. An *obeah* man or woman works spells and creates potions from roots and other forest plants that can heal or harm. However, they are better known for creating mischief.

Before the advent of modern medicine the healing practitioner was sought out to cure illnesses, using ancient herbal remedies. Today, people are turning back to nature in an attempt to recoup knowledge about the medicinal properties of native plants, which flourish in the mountains, jungles and domestic gardens.

GOVERNMENT

St Lucia is governed by a multi-party parliamentary democracy based on the British model and led by an elected prime minister. There are two main political parties: the St Lucia Labour Party (SLP) and the United Workers' Party (UWP). A House of Assembly made up of 17 members is elected for a five-year term and the island's Governor General appoints the 11-member Senate.

St Lucia was declared independent on 22 February 1979 but remains a member of the Commonwealth with Queen Elizabeth II as head of state, represented by the Governor General. Immediately following independence the country voted the SLP into office, in effect snubbing the UWP, which had played an important role in the negotiations that helped establish modern St Lucia. John Compton was the leader of the UWP, pre-independence premier and the first prime minister.

However, the UWP won the 1982 election and the subsequent two elections, which kept them in power until 1997, when a mixture of domestic problems and disillusionment led to a resounding victory for the SLP. Led by Dr Kenny Anthony, the SLP won 16 of the 17 seats and remained in power until 2006, when the electorate opted for change, voting for the UWP (11 seats). The party was again led by Sir John Compton, who came out of retirement, aged 81, to take up office. He

National symbols
Sydney Bagshaw designed the St Lucia coat of arms. The artist Dunstan St Omer designed the National Flag (a royal blue rectangle containing a black, white and yellow triangle).

First Communion

was unable to see out his mandate and died in September 2007 after a series of strokes. He was replaced as Prime Minister by Stephenson King. The next elections are due by December 2011.

The island, which is divided into 11 districts, has no army but there is a special paramilitary unit within the police force.

AGRICULTURE

The St Lucian economy was based on agriculture. First came the rise of sugar plantations, supported, from the late 17th to mid-19th century, by the slave trade, which provided a work force. After the Emancipation Act of 1834, which came into force four years later, slavery was phased out, but there was little change on the land. St Lucia was never a big sugar producer and by the mid-20th century cheap beet sugar and competition from islands such as Barbados forced the island to look to other industries, such as tourism and agricultural crops as a source of income.

Above: Sir John Compton, the first prime minister after Independence in 1979
Below: the modern waterfront, Castries

The banana industry, once estimated to be worth millions of dollars, used to employ the biggest percentage of the St Lucian work force but times have changed. The large plantations in the valleys have passed into the hands of small farmers, most with holdings of 2 hectares (5 acres) or less, who export mainly to the United Kingdom. St Lucia remains

the largest banana producer in the Windward Islands but production has dropped. Many farmers who were cultivating the hillsides and marginal lands have been forced to abandon the crop. This slump is due to a combination of factors, from crop vulnerability to tropical storm damage and competition pushing prices down.

Another crop that brings in revenue is cassava, and there are continuing attempts by small farmers to diversify, looking to crops such as coconuts, mangoes, cocoa and avocados. Overall, agriculture accounts for around 5 percent of the island's gross domestic product (GDP).

TOURISM

St Lucia's economy depends primarily on revenue from tourism, offshore banking and banana production, with some contribution from a relatively diverse manufacturing sector. All sectors of the economy have benefited from infrastructure improvements in roads, communications, water supply, sewerage and port facilities. These improvements, combined with a stable political environment and educated work force, have attracted a steady flow of investment in tourism, with new hotels being built.

Contributing 80 percent to St Lucia's GDP, services, including tourism, have surpassed agriculture as the island's top foreign exchange earner. More than half the work force is employed in the tourist industry and service sector, from roadside vendors to tour guides, taxi drivers to hotel managers. It is a buoyant sector with more than 310,000 people visiting the tiny island each year, not including 620,000 cruise ship passengers.

FISHING

The St Lucian coast is scattered with small fishing villages where whole communities rely on the fruits of the sea to make a living. Fishing is a tough but financially rewarding business that is very important to the island's economy. From Soufrière to Anse La Raye, Laborie and elsewhere, fisher-

Fairtrade Bananas
Banana growers in the Windward Islands benefit from the Fairtrade scheme. It enables small farm owners to pay decent wages to their workers and protect their environment without resorting to heavy use of agrochemicals. They produce less than half the quantity of bananas per hectare produced in the intensive, corporate-owned plantations of Latin America, but in the fragile island ecosystems such levels of output would be unsustainable. At a time when international competition is fierce, with the end of EU quotas because of WTO rulings, the Fairtrade scheme is vital to the survival of St Lucian banana farmers. In 2007, Sainsbury's supermarket announced that all the bananas it sells would be fairly traded and that 100 million, or 75 percent of the total crop, would come from St Lucia.

St Lucia produces the largest banana crop in the Windward Islands

Heritage Tourism
St Lucia promotes heritage tourism aimed at attracting visitors to its natural sites, such as the rainforest and its waterfalls, pristine coral reefs and old estates. The aim is to ensure community participation, cultural preservation, managed development and sustainable tourism.

men work in waters that are protected not just from over-fishing but from the encroaching effects of tourism. Fresh fish such as tuna, dolphin (mahi-mahi or dorado), kingfish, flying fish and snapper end up on the menus of St Lucia's restaurants. The island's waters are also good for crayfish (spiny lobster) in season; traditional methods using lobster pots and baskets are still sometimes used.

ENVIRONMENT AND WILDLIFE

St Lucia has a thriving forest covering 77 sq km (30 sq miles) and a greater biodiversity than neighbouring Dominica. Although a large proportion of native forest was cut down for plantation crops in colonial times, much of the remaining rainforest is protected now to safeguard the island's water supply and wildlife. Fresh water cascades through the mountains, the rivers and streams feeding the land below. Protected within a group of nature reserves, including Edmond Forest Reserve and Quilesse Forest Reserve, the dense forest is populated by indigenous and transplanted species, with flowering trees such as the immortelle or African tulip tree providing bursts of colour.

Rare birds and wildlife include the national bird, the St Lucian parrot, the St Lucia oriole, the red-billed tropic bird and the St Lucia black finch. Nature trails through the forest may also

A fisherman and seine

reveal the guinea pig-like creature called an agouti, an iguana or a mongoose. Native to the island are the boa constrictor and the poisonous fer-de-lance snake, rarely seen because the creatures populate the dry scrub areas on the east coast not usually explored by walkers.

On the west coast are the fertile valleys of Roseau and Cul de Sac where many of the banana plantations are located. In contrast, the north of the island is drier, with cacti proliferating in the scrubland.

Learning from the mistakes made during rapid tourism development elsewhere, St Lucia has been mindful to preserve the natural environment that attracts many visitors. Divers and snorkellers flock to the diverse sea life of the coral reefs that border the western and southern areas of the island. The reefs form part of four designated marine reserves that also protect the livelihood of local fishermen. Along the east coast mainland close to the Fregate Islands are shallow reefs and red mangroves. The protected area is a nesting site for the frigate bird, among others. The beach at Grande Anse in the northeast is a nesting ground of the leatherback turtle (*Demochelys coriacea*), the world's largest marine turtle, and an endangered species.

PRESERVING THE WHIPTAIL LIZARD

The St Lucia whiptail lizard (*Cnemidophorus vanzoi*) is not only endemic to St Lucia but is the only whiptail found in the Eastern Caribbean. The males sport the colours of the St Lucian flag: black, white, blue and yellow. Cats, rats and mongooses decimated the population until by the 1960s only a few lizards remained on the Maria Islands offshore.

In the 1990s the Forestry Department and the Durrell Wildlife Conservation Trust began a program to introduce the whiptail to other predator-free offshore islands. A satellite colony on Praslin Island was hugely successful and this was followed in 2008 by introducing whiptails to Rat Island, on the west coast off Castries, in order to widen the gene pool. A further colony on Dennery Island is planned.

Below: a colourful angelfish, just one of the many species to be seen when diving

HISTORICAL HIGHLIGHTS

BC 500 Amerindians from South America arrive, the hunter-gatherer Ciboney people from the north of the continent being the first.

AD 200–400 Arawak-speaking Amerindians follow the same path, dated from shards of pottery unearthed by digs.

800–1000 The Kalinago, later known as Caribs, arrive; they settle on the island they call Hewanorra ('land of the iguana').

1550s The pirate François Le Clerc, or Jambe de Bois, is believed to be the first European to try to settle St Lucia.

1605 An English ship, *Olive Branch*, lands at Vieux Fort after being blown off course en route to Guiana (Guyana). Of the 67 survivors only 19 are left a month later; they escape in an Amerindian dugout canoe.

1627 St Lucia appears in a document for the first time as one of the territories granted to the Earl of Carlisle. There are no immediate attempts to settle the land.

1635 The French establish a colony in St Lucia, making a counter-claim that the land was granted to M. d'Esnambuc by Cardinal Richelieu in 1626.

1638 Captain Judlee (also known as Major Judge and Jadlee) lands with 300 men. This is the first serious English attempt to colonise St Lucia. The English stay for 18 months and live alongside the Amerindians until a dispute in 1640 leads to many deaths on both sides. The English survivors flee.

1643 The French appoint a governor to the island, M. Rousselan. Married to an Amerindian, he makes peace and establishes the first permanent settlement.

1651 The French West India Company claims the island.

1659 The British and the French fight over St Lucia because of its strategic position. The dispute continues for 150 years, during which time the island changes hands 14 times.

1664 Francis Lord Willoughby, Governor of Barbados, sends 1,000 troops and 600 Amerindians from a base on a neighbouring island to St Lucia. The settlement fails and is abandoned by 1666.

1666 The French attempt to re-take the island but are thwarted by troops from Lord Willoughby's base on Barbados.

1667 The Peace of Breda cedes St Lucia to the French.

1672 Francis Lord Willoughby, Governor of Barbados, St Vincent and Dominica, is appointed governor of St Lucia. The French occupy the island.

1674 The French West India Company closes. St Lucia is annexed to France and becomes a dependency of Martinique.

1686 Another British attempt to take the island is rebuffed by French settlers.

1722 Treaty of Choc declares St Lucia neutral, calls for the French and British forces and nationals to withdraw until the governments agree on the island's future. However, French, British and Irish settlers who operate estates refuse to leave.

1744 The Governor-General of Martinique, Marquis de Champigny, sets up a garrison.

1746 Soufrière is established as the capital under the French.

1748 St Lucia is again declared neutral in the Treaty of Aix-la-Chapelle. The island remains under French control.

1762 Admiral George Rodney invades and takes St Lucia, but it is returned to the French under the Treaty of Paris in 1763. The French introduce sugar cane industry in 1765.

1782 Admiral Rodney destroys the French fleet in the Battle of the Saints off the Windward Islands.

1789 The French Revolution begins; unrest has implications for the colonies.

1796 British troops, led by General Sir Ralph Abercrombie, land at Longueville Bay, Choc Bay and Anse La Raye and beat French resistance. Fire devastates Castries.

1802 Treaty of Amiens ends Seven Years' War and returns St Lucia to the French.

1814 St Lucia is ceded to the British in the Treaty of Paris.

1838 Following the Act of 1834, slavery is abolished in British territories.

1927 Fire destroys most of Castries.

1929 The first airport is built on the island at Castries (called Vigie and later renamed George F. L. Charles Airport).

1939 The first trade union is formed, later becoming the St Lucia Labour Party (SLP).

1948 Fire destroys most of Castries; it is the subject of a poem by Derek Walcott.

1951 Universal adult suffrage is established in the British colonies.

1958–62 St Lucia joins short-lived West Indies Federation; it fails when Jamaica and Trinidad and Tobago break away.

1964 John Compton, leader of the United Workers Party (UWP), is installed as premier where he stays until independence in 1979.

1967 St Lucia introduces internal self-government as an Associated State of the United Kingdom. Sir Frederick Clarke is sworn in as St Lucia's first Governor.

1979 Granted full independence, while remaining part of the British Commonwealth. The St Lucia Labour Party (SLP) wins the first post-independence election. Sir Arthur Lewis is awarded the Nobel Prize for economics.

1992 Castries-born writer Derek Walcott is awarded the Nobel Prize for literature.

1994 Tropical Storm Debby hits St Lucia, 66cm (26 inches) of rain falls in seven hours. Four people die and 24 are injured.

1997 The World Trade Organisation (WTO) declares the EU-Caribbean special trade agreements unfair and illegal. The SLP win the election and again in 2001.

2003 Parliament votes to withdraw from Britain's Privy Council. CARICOM (Caribbean Community and Common Market) establishes a Caribbean Court of Justice.

2005 The Pitons are declared a UNESCO World Heritage Site.

2006 Sir John Compton leads the UWP to electoral victory but dies a year later.

2007 Hurricane Dean destroys 60 percent of the banana crop.

2010 Rain associated with Hurricane Tomas causes mudslides in the Soufrière area which kill 14 people.

2011 Elections due.

Map
on page
24

1: Castries and Environs

Derek Walcott Square – Minor Basilica of the Immaculate Conception – Central Market – Port Castries – Folk Research Centre– Morne Fortune Historic Area

Honourable St Lucian
Born in Castries in 1930, Derek Walcott trained as a painter and writer and studied at the University of the West Indies in Jamaica. In 1953 he moved to Trinidad where, in 1959, he founded the Trinidad Theatre Workshop. In 1981 he set up the Boston Playwrights Theatre at Boston University, where he worked as Professor of Literature until his retirement in 2007. His works include *The Castaway* in 1965, collected Poems 1948–84, the epic *Omeros* in 1990, the play *Odyssey* in 1993 and *Tiepolo's Hound* in 2000.

Preceding pages: view of Soufrière from the Pitons
Below: Vendors' Arcade

St Lucia's capital, Castries, which lies on the western side of the island, has a population of 67,000. It has been razed and rebuilt four times over the years, leaving few old buildings with historic or architectural value. But even though much of the town is made up of nondescript modern buildings, Castries still has character and vibrancy. The attractive harbour is always busy with craft of all sizes.

Visitors who arrive in St Lucia by air will often have their first glimpse of Castries from the road on the drive to their hotel. The lucky ones will enter the city via the Morne on the southern outskirts, looking down over the colourful, sprawling urban area that is Castries and its natural port. At night the view is magical, too, with the town's lights sparkling like thousands of fireflies.

By day, Castries is alive with activity, especially on Saturday when the market is awash with local people doing their weekly shopping and curious tourists enjoying the atmosphere and searching for souvenirs. If there are cruise ships in port, then Castries virtually bulges at the seams.

A tour of Castries can be easily negotiated on foot, as the central area is compact, but a taxi or hire car is recommended when you explore the sights such as Morne Fortune on the southern outskirts.

AN HONOURABLE SQUARE

★★ Derek Walcott Square ❶ sits at the heart of the capital bordered by Brazil, Laborie, Micoud and Bourbon streets. This quiet square, its well-kept, small green space scattered with a few mature trees, was called Place d'Armes in the 18th century, when it was the site of public executions around the time of the French Revolution. By the late 20th century, the square had undergone two name changes: it was called

Columbus Square until 1993, when it was renamed in honour of Castries-born poet and playwright Derek Walcott, who won the Nobel Prize for literature in 1992. He also won the T.S. Eliot Prize in 2011 for *White Egrets* (2010), and since 2010 has been Professor of Poetry at the University of Essex in the UK.

Enter the square either through the west gates on Bourbon Street, facing the beautiful Carnegie Library building, or at Laborie Street, which runs from Jeremie Street at its north end to Brazil Street at the southern end. A tall samaan tree with branches laden with epiphytes stands near the east gates on the Laborie Street side of the square; it is believed to be more than 400 years old and offers some shady relief from the tropical sun. A paved pathway runs through the middle of the grassy square linking a memorial obelisk and plaque to the bandstand at the opposite end. The memorial at the west side of the square honours the memory of St Lucians who fought and died in both World Wars.

JAZZ ON THE SQUARE

This little square is the site of 'Jazz on the Square', a popular event that attracts visitors and locals who gather here for a daily dose of free music during the St Lucia Jazz Festival, which is held in May.

Star Attraction
● Derek Walcott Square

Below: Derek Walcott Square
Bottom: Carnegie Library

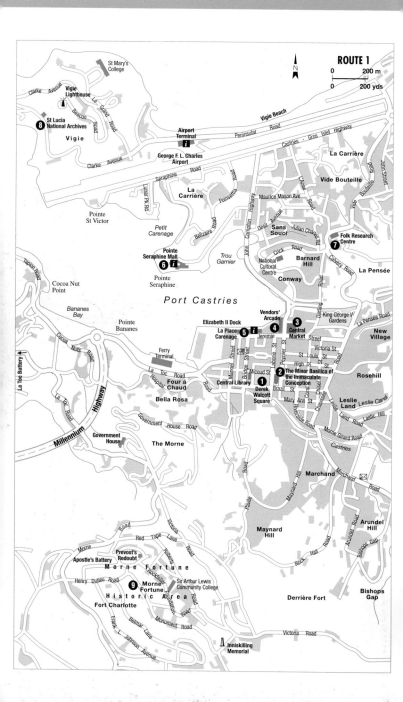

ROUTE 1

0   200 m
0   200 yds

N

St Mary's College

Vigie Lighthouse

Clarke Avenue

Le Gérard Road

Beacon Road

St Lucia National Archives 8

Vigie

Vigie Beach

Airport Terminal

Castries – Gros Islet Highway

Peninsular Road

George F. L. Charles Airport

La Carrière

Clarke Avenue

Seraphine Road

Lunar Pk Rd

La Carrière

Vide Bouteille

John Street

Vide Bouteille Road

Poinsettia Road

Bélizaire Road

John Compton Highway

Désir Avenue

Maurice Mason Ave

L'Anse Road

Pointe St Victor

Petit Carenage

Sans Souci

Julian Charles Rd

Folk Research Centre 7

Pointe Seraphine Mall 6 i

Pointe Seraphine

Trou Garnier

Crick Road

National Cultural Centre

Barnard Hill

Conway

Calvary Road

La Pensée

Cocoa Nut Point

Tapion Road

Bananes Bay

Cocoa Nuts Road

Pointe Bananes

Port Castries

Vendors' Arcade

Central Market 3

King George V Gardens

La Pensée Road

Elizabeth II Dock

La Place Carenage 5 i

Jeremie

Laborie St

Peynier St

Brazil St

New Village

Ferry Terminal

La Toc Road

Hospital Road

Manoel Street

Bridge Street

Micoud St

The Minor Basilica of the Immaculate Conception 2

Central Market 4

Victoria St

St Louis St

High St

Rosehill

La Toc Battery

La Toc Road

Four à Chaud

Bella Rosa

Central Library

Derek Walcott Square 1

Mary Ann St

Chaussée

Riverside Road

Leslie Land

Leslie Land Road

Leslie Carrel

Lastic Hill

Millennium Highway

Government House Road

Government House

The Morne

Pavée Road

Morne Girard Road

Castries

Marchand

Marchand Road

Maynard Hill

Maynard Road

Arundel Hill

Arundel Road

Bishops Gap

Morne Fortune

Red Tape Lane

Victoria Road

Roberts Road

Rockette Road

Apostle's Battery

Prevost's Redoubt

Henry Dulieu Road

Sir Arthur Lewis Community College

Morne Fortune 9

Historic Area

Fort Charlotte

Monument Road

Frank Johnson Avenue

Belmar Lane

Rock Hall Road

Bishops Gap

Derrière Fort

Victoria Road

Inniskilling Memorial

Office workers often use the bandstand and benches here during their lunch hour. At the centre of the square is a fountain and a little way back towards the bandstand are busts of the island's two Nobel Prize winners: Derek Walcott and economist Sir Arthur Lewis *(see page 32)*.

Star Attraction
● **Castries Cathedral**

A Beautiful Cathedral

On the corner of Laborie and Micoud streets is the Roman Catholic cathedral ★★ **The Minor Basilica of the Immaculate Conception** ➋ (open daily unless Mass is in progress). This has been the site of several churches dating back to the 18th century, but the current building was not completed until 1931. Don't be fooled by the church's shabby exterior; inside there are enough beautiful dark wood pews to seat around 2,000, intricately carved columns and arches, and a stone altar flanked by displays of votive candles, which can also be found near the cathedral's side altars. Yellow light floods the building via decorative windows in the ceiling, which is adorned with a depiction of Catholic saints. Renowned St Lucian artist, Dunstan St Omer, painted the murals on the cathedral walls in 1985 in preparation for a visit by Pope John Paul II the following year. The beautiful paintings reveal the Stations of the Cross

The beautiful interior of the cathedral, the Minor Basilica of the Immaculate Conception

Map on page 24

> **A local staple**
> Cassava is a root vegetable grown throughout St Lucia. The plant is peeled and grated and the juice extracted, before it is dried to produce farine (a fine flour), which is used to make bread or porridge.

Shopping at Pointe Seraphine

with characters inspired by local people. More of the artist's work can be seen in rural churches across the island *(see Jacmel, page 56)*. In 2005, St Omer and his son, Giovanni, created 12 magnificent stained glass windows that were installed on either side of the cathedral.

As you leave the cathedral on Laborie Street, to your left is Brazil Street, which has several buildings dating back to the late 19th century. Though fading, the wooden structures retain some lovely gingerbread fretwork detail on their balconies. These and the buildings behind were the only ones of their kind to survive Castries' last great fire in 1948.

CENTRAL MARKET

One of the only other places to escape the flames in 1948 was the old ★★**Central Market** ❸ situated north of Jeremie Street towards John Compton Highway. Built of iron in 1894, the original market shelter is where you will find the town clock and a modern annexe. Wander through the noisy market where vendors from rural areas sell local produce, such as fruit, vegetables, cassava, cocoa sticks, pepper sauces, spices and basketwork. Across the road on Peynier Street is the ★★**Vendors' Arcade** ❹, which backs on to the waterfront; you can find an array of souvenirs and gifts including inexpensive, colourful T-shirts, beach wraps and some very good basketwork, in both traditional and modern styles. Shop around for a good price and don't feel that you have to buy, no matter how persuasive the sales pitch may be.

SHOP TILL YOU DROP

Head west from the Arcade along Jeremie Street to La Place Carenage, the duty-free shopping mall. The waterfront is on the right-hand side behind the mall and other buildings that include the district's fire station and central police station. On the opposite side of the busy road there is a small bookshop, which also has a good stock of local newspapers and international magazines.

★ **La Place Carenage** ❺ (Mon–Fri 9am–5pm, Sat 9am–2pm, also Sun if a cruise ship is in town), which lies adjacent to Castries' cruise ship dock, has an entrance on Jeremie Street. The mall has a selection of shops selling crafts and souvenirs, boutiques and art galleries. The mall also has a small interpretative facility, the **Desmond Skeete Animation Centre**, which has displays of ancient Amerindian artefacts and an audio tour.

Across the harbour and reached by a regular water taxi service is the larger and more upscale **Pointe Seraphine** ❻ duty-free shopping mall (Mon–Sat 9am–5pm, also Sun if a cruise ship is in town). This remote but expansive shopping haven is generally quiet during the week because of its distance from the centre of town, but is busier at the weekend and even more so when a cruise ship is anchored at the dock next door. If you don't want to take the inexpensive ferry to cross the water then your best bet is to jump in a taxi for the short drive around the harbour. Travel along John Compton Highway heading north towards George F.L. Charles Airport (formerly known as Vigie Airport), turn left at the fish market complex and continue to the shopping mall. The walk from here to Castries centre isn't that long, but it can seem so, especially in the heat.

Star Attractions
● **Central Market**
● **Vendors' Arcade**
● **La Place Carenage**

Below: waiting for a water taxi in Castries
Bottom: a cruise ship dwarfs the dock at Pointe Seraphine

PORT CASTRIES AND VIGIE PENINSULA

The Port of Castries is a busy working harbour where container ships can be seen unloading their contents on to the dock at the North Wharf, adjacent to the Place Carenage duty-free shopping mall. When cruise ships are in the harbour they dominate all other vessels and even the surrounding buildings. Fishing boats painted the colours of the rainbow can be seen dodging the big ships to get in and out of their harbour in Trou Garnier, while yachts sail in and out of Petit Carenage.

Heading west along La Toc Road you come to the ferry terminal, from where the L'Express des Iles ferry operates a regular and fast service to Martinique, Dominica, Guadeloupe and the outer French islands *(see Practical Information on page 107)*.

The port has two major anchorages at Castries City and another, Vigie Creek, a little further out near the airport. A guide light on Vigie Hill aids the approach to port, but visiting yachts are better off clearing customs at Rodney Bay Marina or Marigot Harbour *(see page 39)*.

Above: the military cemetery at Choc Bay
Below: the Folk Research Centre, a cultural archive

CULTURAL ARCHIVE

The ★★★ **Folk Research Centre** ❼ (Plas Wichès Folklò, Mount Pleasant; Mon–Fri 8.30am–4.30pm;

tel: 452 2279; www.stluciafolk.org) stands near L'Anse Road off the Gros Islet Highway, east of the harbour and north of the town centre. The Centre is in a 19th-century colonial estate house formerly owned by the Devaux family. Today it houses a cultural archive and a small museum containing a reproduction of an indigenous dwelling called a ti-kay hut, some old ceramics, and a variety of traditional musical instruments including a *chak-chak*, named after the sound the seeds inside it make when shaken.

On the first floor, the library has an excellent collection of history books, reference material, audio-visual recordings and priceless photographs. This is the island's best folk history and culture study centre, which was set up to promote and preserve traditional customs and the Kwéyòl language and art. It offers Kwéyòl language classes, school programmes, translation services, orthography, folk art production and exhibitions. There are numerous events and performances during La Rose, La Marguerite and Kwéyòl festivals and at Christmas, but it is especially busy in October during Creole heritage month. Jounen Kwéyòl at the end of October is a community-based celebration of food, music and folk traditions, coinciding with the Journée International du Créole.

MILITARY CEMETERY

Back on Gros Islet Highway head east to the roundabout and take Peninsular Road towards the airport, a small landing strip for Caribbean inter-island and domestic flights. As you round the corner to join Peninsular Road, with the airport runway on your left, you will see the raised white tombstones and monuments in the small military cemetery created for the men of the West India Regiment. South of the runway is a complex that houses government offices and the Pointe Seraphine shopping mall, while the public Vigie Beach runs alongside the road on the right. The water here is calm and there is a beach with a few benches for picnickers.

Star Attraction
● **Folk Research Centre**

Sail on a pirate ship
For many years would-be pirates have been entertained on the tall ship Brig *Unicorn*, used in the filming of the epic television mini-series about slavery, *Roots*. The TV series was based on the book of the same name by the late Alex Haley, which was published in 1976. The ship also appeared in the film *Pirates of the Caribbean*. Built in 1946 as a replica of a ship from 1850, it is currently out of service as a tourist vessel. Temporarily replaced by the Nova Scotia tall ship *Liana's Ransom*, you can still be a pirate for the day and sail the west coast of the island.

The candle-like flowers of pachystachys (pachystachys lutea) are a familiar sight

Map on page 24

Below: Government House
Bottom: ubiquitous hibiscus

A MILITARY STRONGHOLD

Continue west along the Vigie Peninsula heading up the steep hill towards the French Embassy and the St Lucia National Archives, which are housed in 19th-century military buildings with small verandas. The entire peninsula was once a military stronghold and the barracks and other buildings have been restored.

The **St Lucia National Archives** ❽ (Clarke Avenue; Mon–Fri 8.30am–4.30pm; tel: 452 1654) is a valuable historical resource containing books, newspapers and journals, many stored on microfilm. The National Archives Portrait Gallery, opened in 2010, houses a changing exhibition of photographs and portraits of eminent St Lucians from all walks of life, some painted by the local artists Cedric George and Dunstan St Omer.

BEACON

Vigie Lighthouse stands at the end of Beacon Road on the peninsula, on the northern side of the city harbour. The light from the red lantern at the top of the 11m (36ft) white tower, built in 1914, can be seen about 50km (30 miles) out to sea. The lighthouse overlooks military barracks, 18th-century ruins and other historic buildings managed by the National Trust. From here on a clear day there are spectacular views of the southern and northern coasts, and Martinique.

In another restored military barracks, north of the lighthouse and close to the top of Le Grand Road before you reach the radio mast, is St Mary's College Catholic boys' school.

ON THE MORNE

The historic Morne area, which is on the way to Fort Charlotte *(see page 32),* is accessible from the southern end of the centre of Castries.

Head west out of town along La Toc Road, with the harbour on the right-hand side, and up the hill in the direction of the Millennium Highway.

Drive for just a few minutes to reach the studio of **Bagshaws of St Lucia** (Mon–Fri 8.30am–

4pm; tours Sat–Sun by appointment; tel: 452 6039; www.bagshawsstlucia.com). The factory uses traditional silk-screen methods to produce colourful prints on fabric, with motifs inspired by island flora and fauna. It is worth taking one of the organised tours on offer, which provide a lively explanation of the printing process and details about Bagshaws. The company also has shopping outlets at La Carenage and Pointe Seraphine in Castries (*see page 27 for opening times*), and another at Hewanorra Airport.

Next door, Bagshaws have restored **La Toc Battery** (tours by appointment; tel: 452 6039), a fine example of a 19th-century battlement with wonderful views and a pretty garden. Built by the British, La Toc has cannons, underground tunnels and munitions storage rooms where valuable artefacts can be seen. There is also a display of some 900 old bottles and other artefacts, found by scuba divers in Castries' harbour.

Travelling further up the hill take a detour along Government House Road, which branches off to the left towards **Government House**, the official residence of the island's Governor General. Built in 1895, the colonial building is not open to the public. However, there is a small museum on the side of the residence, **Le Pavillon Royal Museum** (Tue and Thur 10am–noon and 2–4pm; tours by appointment;

> **Workers' champion**
> George Frederick Lawrence Charles was St Lucia's first Minister of Education and Social Affairs and first Chief Minister. He came to prominence in 1945 when he championed the cause of striking construction workers who were employed to build an extension to the airport. Charles later became the secretary of the St Lucia Workers Co-operative Union. Knighted in 1998, the airport in Castries was renamed in his honour and a sculpture of the trade unionist was erected there in 2002. He was honoured with a state funeral following his death in 2004.

A cannon at the ready at Fort Charlotte

Map on page 24

tel: 452 2481; www.governmenthouse.lc/le-pavillon-royal-museum), where visitors can view important artefacts and documents.

HISTORIC MORNE FORTUNE

Back on the main road, continue up to the 29-hectare (72-acre) ★★★ **Morne Fortune Historic Area** ❾ on top of the hill, where you will find the old military buildings of **Fort Charlotte**. The French began building the original fortress in 1768, choosing 260m (850ft) -high Morne Fortune because of its unmatched vantage point of the harbour.

When they took control of St Lucia in 1814, the British continued the work and strengthened the fortifications. It was they who named it Fort Charlotte. The fort remained an important defensive base until early in the 20th century. The military barracks and other buildings have been restored and converted into the administrative headquarters of the OECS (Organisation of Eastern Caribbean States). The buildings also house the Sir Arthur Lewis Community College, named after the island's first Nobel Prize winner, who is buried here.

Nearby are the ruins of Apostle's Battery, with a large mounted cannon, built in 1890 to support the fortress, as well as the lookout point at Prevost's

The Brigands

In 1794, the new French Republic granted freedom to enslaved Africans in its foreign territories. But when St Lucia was again brought under British influence the newly emancipated islanders, fearing they would be returned to bondage, banded together, joined by a number of French army deserters, to create l'Armée Française dans les Bois. The rebels – called Brigands by their enemies – led a campaign of resistance across the island. In 1795 they took control of the fortifications on Pigeon Island, but victory was short-lived. In 1796 British forces defeated and captured them at Morne Fortune.

A woodcarver displays his work

Redoubt, a French construction dating from 1782.

At the southern boundaries of the fort complex is the **Royal Inniskilling Fusiliers Memorial**, a monument to the soldiers who battled for this position against the Brigands *(see margin box, page 32)* and the French in 1796. The monument also marks one of the best viewpoints on the Morne, affording stunning coastal views to Pigeon Island in the north and as far as the Pitons on the west coast.

Star Attractions
● Morne Fortune
● Eudovic's Art Studio
● Caribelle Batik

AN ARTISTIC COMMUNITY

The hills around the Morne Fortune district are dotted with hotels and restaurants. Here, too, is a small artistic community that includes the Goodlands workshop of the St Lucian sculptor and woodcarver Vincent Joseph Eudovic *(see page 92)*. At ★★ **Eudovic's Art Studio and Gallery** (Mon–Fri 7.30am–4.30pm, Sat–Sun until 3pm; tel: 452 2747; http://eudovicart.com) woodcarvers produce smooth abstract carvings. The works are made from the ancient roots and stumps of the laurier canelle, laurier mabouey, teak, mahogany and red and white cedar.

All of the family are artists, but it is not just the wood creations and other artwork that attract visitors. The Eudovics also run a guesthouse and a restaurant on the property.

Howelton House, the home of ★★ **Caribelle Batik** (Mon–Fri 8am–4pm, Sat 8am–noon, Sun if a cruise ship is in port; tel: 452 3785), is a fine example of Victorian architecture with a Caribbean twist. The pretty building on Old Victoria Road has been carefully restored and houses a batik studio and print shop, which uses Indonesian techniques to create vibrant designs on British and sea-island cotton. The fabric, printed with images of St Lucia's flora and fauna, such as colourful heliconia, is then made into clothing, wall hangings and souvenirs that are sold in Caribelle's shop. Visitors can enjoy light refreshments and local ice creams on the patio where there are views over Castries and across to Martinique.

Art from indigenous wood at Eudovic's Art Studio

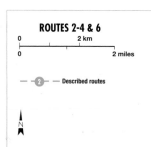

ROUTES 2-4 & 6

0   2 km
0   2 miles

— ② — **Described routes**

N

CARIBBEAN

SEA

Labrellotte

Labrellotte

Masson

Rat Island

D'Estrées Point

George F. L. Charles Airport ✈

Port Castries

Castries

Coubaril Point

Ciceron Point

*Grande
Cul de Sac
Bay*   ○ Ciceron

Bananes Point

Morne
St Joseph   ○ Soucis

Marigot Point

Marigot Bay   Marigot   ○ La Croix
                                   Maingot

Marigot Bay   ○ Barre
                                     Duchaussee

**Roseau Valley
Banana Plantation** ★

**St Lucia
Distillers**

Roseau Bay   **Roseau Valley   ○ Jacmel
Massacre   Banana Plantation**

                                   ○ Vanard

Anse La Raye ★

Anse Galet   **La Sikwi
                Sugar Mill** ★
Pointe la Ville

Anse Cochon   *Grande Rivière de L'Anse La Raye*   Durandeau

Anse La Voutte
Jambette Point

Plas Kassav ★   Anse
                    La Verdure

Canaries ○

Anse La Liberté   *Canaries*   **Grand Bois
Soufrière ◄   Forest**   ○ Millet

Roseau

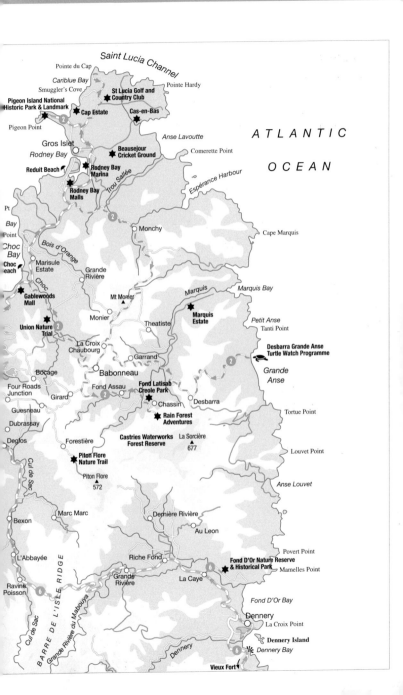

Saint Lucia Channel

Pointe du Cap
Cariblue Bay
Smuggler's Cove
Pointe Hardy
Pigeon Island National
Historic Park & Landmark
St Lucia Golf and
Country Club
Cap Estate
Cas-en-Bas
Pigeon Point
Anse Lavoutte
Gros Islet
Rodney Bay
Comerette Point
Beausejour
Cricket Ground
Reduit Beach
Rodney Bay
Marina
Espérance Harbour
Rodney Bay
Malls
Pt
Bay
Point
Cape Marquis
Choc
Bay
Bois d'Orange
Choc
Beach
Marisule
Estate
Monchy
Grande
Rivière
Marquis Bay
Gablewoods
Mall
Mt Morne
Marquis
Union Nature
Trial
Monier
Marquis
Estate
Theatiste
Petit Anse
Tanti Point
La Croix
Chaubourg
Garrand
Desbarra Grande Anse
Turtle Watch Programme
Bocage
Babonneau
Grande
Anse
Four Roads
Junction
Fond Assau
Fond Latisab
Creole Park
Girard
Chassim
Desbarra
Guesneau
Rain Forest
Adventures
Tortue Point
Dubrassay
Deglos
Castries Waterworks
Forest Reserve
La Sorcière
677
Forestière
Louvet Point
Piton Flore
Nature Trail
Piton Flore
572
Anse Louvet
Marc Marc
Dernière Rivière
Bexon
Au Leon
Povert Point
L'Abbayée
Riche Fond
Fond D'Or Nature Reserve
& Historical Park
Mamelles Point
Ravine
Poisson
Grande
Rivière
La Caye
Fond D'Or Bay
Dennery
La Croix Point
Dennery Island
Dennery Bay
Dennery
Vieux Fort

ATLANTIC

OCEAN

BARRE DE L'ISLE RIDGE
Cul de Sac
Grande Rivière du Mabouya
Trou Sallée

Map
on pages
34–5

2: Rodney Bay and the Far North

Castries – Rodney Bay – Reduit Beach – Gros Islet – Pigeon Island National Landmark – Pointe du Cap – Babonneau – Grande Anse

👁 **Rodney Bay**
Rodney Bay is named after Admiral George Brydges Rodney, who claimed St Lucia for the British in 1762 and later established a naval base at nearby Pigeon Island.

The coastal region to the north of Castries is the island's foremost resort area with sheltered bays, upmarket hotels, quaint fishing communities, a marina, shopping malls and historic landmarks. In the northeast turtles nest, while rural life inland continues much as it has for generations.

From Castries head north on John Compton Highway passing the government offices on the right-hand side, with the port on the left. At the end of the highway turn on to the Castries–Gros Islet Highway, which runs parallel to the George F.L. Charles airport runway and the Peninsular Road on the other side leading to the airport. At the roundabout take the second exit for Rodney Bay.

The journey north to the Rodney Bay resort area and beyond from the capital is straightforward. Bus No. 1A follows a route to Gros Islet from the Castries bus terminus on Darling Road behind Central Market *(see page 26)*. The roads along this coast are good, if winding, so driving a hire car is hindered only by the lack of signage.

US-STYLE SHOPPING

The highway is flanked by tree-shaded hotels which hug the shoreline. About 3km (2 miles) from Castries is **Gablewoods Mall**, clearly visible from the road. This precinct in a district called Sunny Acres includes a supermarket, boutiques, post office, bank, restaurants, a pharmacy, souvenir and gift shops and a large branch of the island's own Sunshine Bookshop (tel: 452 3419). There is plenty of car parking.

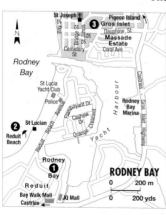

RODNEY BAY

0   200 m
0   200 yds

CALM WATERS

West of the highway, several more hotels and restaurants nestle in the curve of **Choc Bay** and along Choc Beach, which is lapped by the calm waters of the Caribbean. At Choc roundabout is the island's cinema, with ten screens showing all the latest international movie releases. Continuing north, the highway passes above the Choc River and the road winds on through the Quarter of Gros Islet and its undulating hills. To the west, in Bois d'Orange, residences and a hotel are scattered around the hill overlooking **Labrellotte Bay**. From here there are splendid views along the coast and over the bay, which has two good diving sites: Labrellotte Point and Masson Point.

Off the highway, away from the main tourist centres of Castries, Rodney Bay and Gros Islet, the roads in rural St Lucia lack signposts and can be severely potholed, which is why organised tours are a popular option for many visitors.

REDUIT BEACH

The Castries–Gros Islet Highway continues north. Keep an eye out for the Bay Walk Mall on the left-hand side of the road, at ★★ **Rodney Bay ❶**, a former US military base. Taking a left turn at the mall will lead you to Reduit Beach Avenue, where there is a bank with an ATM, lively bars, restaurants and small hotels. At the end of the road is ★★★**Reduit Beach ❷**, one of the best stretches of sand on the island, with places to stay and eat on either side

Star Attractions
● **Rodney Bay**
● **Reduit Beach**

Below: Reduit Beach
Bottom: beachfront rooms at the St Lucian, Reduit Beach

Map on pages 34–5

of the road. The crescent-shaped beach extends as far as Pigeon Island *(see page 40)* further north, although it is not possible to walk the length of it because of shipping access to Rodney Bay marina and The Landings yacht harbour. There is public access to the beach, where visitors can rent sun loungers and umbrellas, indulge in water sports by hiring equipment, or simply enjoy a paddle in the water. In high season, when the hotels are full, and at weekends, when local people visit the beach, it can become crowded, but there is usually enough space for everyone. If you are looking for tranquillity, come on a weekday in the off season. Licensed vendors work this beach, but if you are not interested in what they have to sell a polite 'no thank you' is usually all it takes to discourage them.

CUISINE AND CULTURE

Less than a 10-minute walk from the sand, back on Reduit Beach Avenue, there is a choice of bars and restaurants. This is the hip strip for nightlife in St Lucia, being close to hotels, with food outlets serving simple sandwiches, pizza, steak, seafood and Chinese, Indian, Italian and Caribbean cuisine. The hotels also organise entertainment such as crab racing, fire eaters, steel bands or jazz groups and several restaurants have live music on certain nights.

Below: West Coast beaches are good for water sports
Bottom: the sheltered marina at Rodney Bay

SAILORS' CHOICE

The shopping in Rodney Bay is the best on the island, particularly since the 2010 opening of Bay Walk Mall opposite the older JQ Mall. The mall has international designer boutiques, shops selling gifts, books and newspapers, and a casino. There is a supermarket in each Mall and plenty of opportunities for sailors to provision their yachts.

★★**Rodney Bay Marina** and its harbour were created less than half a century ago by an ambitious programme that reclaimed a mangrove swamp. The popular marina is well equipped and is considered to be among the Caribbean's best, with shops, places to eat and drink, and bank facilities. The bars and restaurants in the area host lots of activities that revolve around the **Atlantic Rally for Cruisers** (ARC), a big winter event on the sailing calendar (*see box, page 40*). Yachts from all over the world take part in this annual transatlantic rally, setting sail in November from Las Palmas in Gran Canaria to Rodney Bay in St Lucia. The 2,700-nautical mile journey takes anything from 12 to 24 days, and festivities around the marina continue as long as it takes for the vessels to reach their destination.

★★**Gros Islet** ❸ (pronounced *grows ee-lay*), just north of the marina, is a small fishing village that during the week is an antidote to the pace of the busy harbour. However, the hamlet comes alive for a street party on Friday evening.

Single- and two-storey wooden buildings line the streets and while some retain a little faded character most are unimpressive. Most notable is **St Joseph the Worker Roman Catholic Church** at the north end of Bridge Street, on Church Street. It was built in 1926 on the site of an earlier church that was destroyed in the devastating earthquake of 1906. At the end of Dauphine Street, the main road, is Bay Street and a small strip of sand where you are likely to see few people save a handful of fishermen. It is safe to swim here but there are better beaches close by, such as Reduit Beach (*see page 37*) south across the harbour and the Causeway Beach at Pigeon Island National Landmark (*see page 40*).

Star Attractions
● Rodney Bay Marina
● Gros Islet

*Below: dancing at Gros Islet
Bottom: there are plenty of places to dine in Rodney Bay*

Map
on pages
34–5

Turn inland opposite the gas station and beside the new fire station to reach the **Beausejour Cricket Ground**, which hosts international test matches and other events such as the Cricket World Cup in 2007 and the ICC World Twenty20 Championship in 2010.

FRIDAY NIGHT JUMP-UP

Most visitors come to Gros Islet for the **Friday Night Jump-up**, a popular street party when tourists and locals converge on the area. Food and snack vendors line the usually quiet streets, bars and restaurants fling open their doors and sound systems flood the air with the beat of reggae, calypso and soca. This is a good place to enjoy tasty St Lucian dishes, such as locally caught fried fish, chicken or conch, then work off the calories by dancing the night away in the crowded street.

Things don't hot up until after 10pm and festivities go on into the small hours. This is a fun event with a carnival atmosphere as long as you use your common sense: keep your wits about you and always travel in a group. Generally it is pretty safe at the Jump-up, with police, uniformed and plain clothed, on duty.

The Atlantic Rally
The Atlantic Rally for Cruisers is the largest trans-ocean sailing event in the world. It was established in 1986 as a fun race for yachts and crews making their annual winter voyage from the Mediterranean to the Caribbean. Hundreds of vessels sail together across the Atlantic Ocean from the Canary Islands to Rodney Bay Marina, which has been the rally's finishing point since 1990.

Partying at the Friday Night Jump-up

HISTORY OF A NATIONAL LANDMARK

Around the bay from Gros Islet, north on the Gros Islet–Castries Highway, head northwest to ★★★**Pigeon Island National Landmark** (daily 9am–5pm; interpretative centre closed on Sun; entrance fee). This was once a separate island, accessible only by boat, but was joined to the mainland by a man-made causeway, completed in 1972. The causeway encompasses a large Sandals all-inclusive resort and The Landings marina resort, and has offshore snorkelling opportunities. The resorts have claimed part of the sand for guests and more is sectioned off within the park area, but there is still a good stretch open to everyone. There is a small parking area and you can buy snacks from the vendors who trade close to the beach's public access point, which is popular with local people.

Operated by the St Lucia National Trust, Pigeon Island is of significant archaeological and historical importance. It is also the venue for events, including the annual St Lucia Jazz Festival. The hilly land that spans 18 hectares (45 acres) is thought to have been inhabited by Amerindians, who used the island's caves for shelter and grew staple crops such as sweet potatoes and cassava (manioc).

Star Attraction
● **Pigeon Island National Landmark**

Later the site played its part during the 18th- and 19th-century squabbles between European imperialist powers over control of St Lucia. The island's strategic position and usefulness as a lookout made it a popular choice as a military base. French pirates used the island in the 1550s and Admiral Rodney established a naval outpost here in 1780. He sailed from this point to defeat the French forces two years later at the Battle of the Saints, which took place off the Iles des Saintes between Guadeloupe and Dominica.

The Brigands *(see page 32)* captured the island and took control of the fortifications in 1795, forcing the British to abandon St Lucia for a while.

By the early 20th century, Pigeon Island was leased to Napoleon Olivierre from St Vincent, who ran a whaling station. Later, in 1937, the island was leased to Josset Agnes Hutchinson, an actress with the D'Oyly Carte Opera company. There was a hiatus during World War II when

Above: a Gros Islet cook-up
Below: the crescent-shaped beach at Pigeon Island

Map
on pages
34–5

Welcome to
Pigeon Island
National
Landmark

the US established a communications station and a naval air station. In 1947 Hutchinson returned to her house in the south of the island (now a ruin), opening a beachfront restaurant, which attracted a colourful yachting crowd. She finally gave up the lease in 1970 and returned home to Britain in 1976, dying a year later.

Around the Park

Passing through the gates of the park you will be faced with a useful map of the area. The path to the right leads to the ruins of the **Officers' Kitchen** and a little further up the hill is the renovated **Officers' Mess**, a lovely building with a veranda, which houses the small **Interpretative Centre**. Artefacts and historical displays explain the history and natural environment of Pigeon Island, but it is past its best.

The Officers' Mess is also home to the **St Lucia National Trust** (daily 8am–4pm; tel: 452 5005; www.slunatrust.org). The trust was established in 1975 as the result of a campaign to save the Pigeon Island Landmark from being used for a housing development. Its aim is to preserve the natural and cultural heritage of St Lucia, including areas of outstanding natural beauty, and bio-diverse and historic sites such as Pigeon Island, Fregate Island

The ruins of Fort Rodney, Pigeon Island

and Maria Islands. Contact the National Trust office for tours of their properties.

Below the interpretative centre is **The Captain's Cellar Pub**, which remains open after the park closes at 5pm. Wedding ceremonies are held in the white gazebo that stands on an expanse of grass to the left of the path leading to the Officers' Mess and back towards the park gates.

In late spring the property is a popular venue for the St Lucia Jazz Festival (*see page 93*). The stage is usually set up near the Officers' Mess, using the ocean as a beautiful backdrop; crowds arrive early to find a good spot on the grass from which to enjoy the show.

ANIMAL, MINERAL AND VEGETABLE

You can take a guided tour around the park or simply wander along the paths and trails at leisure. There is a variety of flora, fauna and many old buildings, some no more than a collection of stones. The old **Cooperage** has been transformed into public toilet facilities, while an overgrown **military cemetery** holds the graves of old soldiers and sometimes their families, too. On the waterfront, just before you reach the cemetery, is the Jambe de Bois restaurant, a good choice for a drink, an ice cream or a snack. There is a jetty and ferry dock nearby and the lovely beach leads back almost level with the park border and entrance.

LOOKOUT POINT

On a hill, at the southwestern tip of the park, are the ruins of ★★**Fort Rodney**, which had an excellent vantage point. Today, the fort ruins still afford a good view south towards Castries, but the best lookout point is at 110m (361ft) **Signal Peak**. It's a bit of a climb to reach the peak, especially in the hot sun, but it's worth it for the view over neighbouring Gros Islet and far north to the French island of Martinique. There is another lookout at the **Two-Gun Battery** close to the **Soldiers' Barracks**.

Whaling
Napoleon Olivierre, a native of St Vincent and head of a family with a tradition of whaling, was granted permission to establish a whaling station on Pigeon Island in 1909. In the 1920s a small fleet of schooners operated from the bay area around the island, setting up a winch to haul in a whale on the rare occasions that one was caught. There were also facilities to extract the precious, but foul-smelling, oil from the creatures. Government legislation effectively ended whaling on Pigeon Island in 1926.

The renovated Officers' Mess

Map
on pages
34–5

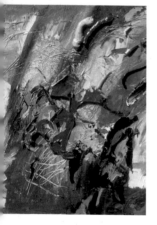

Pigeon Island
Trails around the 18-hectare (45-acre) Pigeon Island National Landmark park are coloured with the blossom of red flamboyant (or flame tree), Brazilian oak and prickly pear cactus, with yellow flowers and purple fruit.

Llewellyn Xavier's art is rich and colourful

CAP ESTATE

Located to the north of Gros Islet, **Cap Estate** lies in hilly land that was once heavily forested. Crops such as tobacco thrived here before the sugar boom of the 18th and 19th centuries resulted in the land being cleared to plant sugar cane. The properties that sit on the former 607-hectare (1,500-acre) plantation today are not farmhouses but the exclusive homes of the wealthy. Residents and guests from the nearby hotels can take advantage of the golf course at the **St Lucia Golf & Country Club** (tel: 450 8523; www.stluciagolf.com), which has a pro shop and club rental.

MULTI-MEDIA ARTIST

In a mansion house on Cap Estate is **Llewellyn Xavier's Studio** (tel: 450 9155; email: xavierl@candw.lc), where the work of the St Lucian multi-media artist can be viewed only by appointment. His art is exhibited in the permanent collections of museums and galleries all over the world including the Smithsonian Institution in Washington, the Metropolitan Museum of Art and the Museum of Art in New York and the National Gallery in Jamaica. Xavier's work can also be seen at the Caribbean Art Gallery (tel: 452 8071), at Rodney Bay Marina, and at Art and Antiques (tel: 451 4150) at Pointe Seraphine in Castries.

The artist's use of oils, watercolours and mixed media reflect the vibrant colours and rich textures of the Caribbean. The artwork *Environmental Fragile*, which was created from cardboard and other recycled material, was commemorated in a postage stamp issue in 2006.

Xavier's first major work in the 1970s was a series of 25 prints dedicated to George Jackson, a young man whose incarceration in America became an international cause célèbre.

THE FAR NORTH

The far north of St Lucia is the driest part of the island and much of the coast is rocky and rough where the waters of the Caribbean Sea meet the

Atlantic Ocean in the St Lucia Channel. There are, however, a couple of pleasant beaches on the northwestern coast, which have inevitably attracted hotel development. The picturesque Bécune Point and the golden sand beach of ★★ **Anse Bécune** form the northern edge of Cap Estate. The beach is dominated by a large, all-inclusive hotel, Smugglers Cove, but there is public access to the beach and sea.

A little further north, there is excellent snorkelling to be had at ★★ **Smuggler's Cove**. With a sheltered beach and rugged cliff landscape, it is often a little quieter than Anse Bécune. Cap Maison Hotel maintains a beach bar here with water sports for guests.

Beyond this is **Cariblue Bay**, a pretty, golden sand beach, which is home to LeSport, another all-inclusive resort.

ROCKY ROADS

At the far north tip of St Lucia is **Pointe du Cap**. At a little under 150m (470ft) high, in a hilly region beyond the Saline Point residential development, Pointe du Cap provides panoramic views across the north coast to Martinique, west to the Caribbean Sea and east to the Atlantic Ocean.

The roads around the northern tip are a warren, with little signposting and lots of pot holes caused

Star Attractions
● Anse Bécune
● Smuggler's Cove

Below: fun in the sea
Bottom: the view from Fort Rodney (see page 43)

Map on pages 34–5

Crayfish

A traditional crayfish pot is made of strips of bamboo lashed together, forming a tube that is laid on the river bed. One end is sealed while the other has a flap to allow access to the creatures caught in the pot. Bait can include fresh coconut, which is used at Fond Latisab Creole Park *(see page 48)*.

by construction vehicles as ever more villa developments are built. Security guards on building sites often prevent traffic passing. If you make it, the view at the end of the route will be well worth it. The sea below the sheer cliffs is rough and the land is dry scrub with cacti a common sight. You can't drive to the lookout point so park below and walk up. To the east is Pointe Hardy where paths for walkers criss-cross the undulating land. The area around Pointe Hardy and north of Cas-en-Bas is part of the large St Lucia Golf and Country Club development.

There are no beaches that can offer safe swimming on this rough, wild and windy Atlantic part of the coast.

CAS-EN-BAS AND ANSE LAVOUTTE

South of Pointe Hardy on the northeast Atlantic side of the island is ★★ **Cas-en-Bas**, known for its collection of quiet beaches. There are no lifeguards, not all the beaches are well maintained and the roads leading to this coast are rough and hard to negotiate, but they are ideal if you want a quiet day away from it all.

To get to Cas-en-Bas, take the road across the golf course, which winds its way to the luxury villa resort, Cotton Bay. The road ends here, blocked by land which is to be developed into

View of LeSport, a resort on Cariblue Bay

another golf course, and you have to continue on foot down the track to the sea. The beaches are in a sheltered and rocky bay and, although the Atlantic waters can be rough, the swimming and snorkelling are usually good. There is a laid-back beach bar, with sun loungers outside and kite-surfing available. Horses on the beach make the sand dirty, but it is pleasant to walk along the rocky coastline.

Further south still is **Anse Lavoutte** and a beach where leatherback turtles nest. Turtle-watch and beach patrols here and at Grande Anse on the east coast are organised by the Desbarra Grande Anse Turtle Watch Group *(see page 51)*.

Star Attraction
● **Cas-en-Bas**

TO THE INTERIOR

From the far north return the way you came, following the route south towards Rodney Bay and the nation's capital. East of Castries and the resort strip is the north's picturesque rural interior that stretches across to the rugged Atlantic coast. This area is rarely visited by the average tourist, but visitors who want to get closer to St Lucian country life will not be disappointed. The land is largely given over to agriculture and small village communities barely affected by tourism development elsewhere.

Travelling from Castries this eastern detour will take you off the Castries–Gros Islet Highway north of Choc Bay and the Bois d'Orange district. The Allan Bousquet Highway leads to the village of Monchy and St Lucia's rural interior: Babonneau, Fond Assau and Desbarra. There are a few basic bed and breakfast places off the beaten track here, which are inexpensive and homely but are only practical if you have transport; taxi fares soon mount up, especially if you do an excursion every day. South of Monchy, through winding roads, is **Babonneau** in the heart of farmland and plantations. The area around Babonneau and Fond Assau is thought to be the place to which the last group of African-born enslaved people were transported, which probably accounts for the strong African tradition that has been retained.

Below: fragrant frangipani (Plumeria rubra)

Map
on pages
34–5

Below: cocoa pods on a tree
Bottom: from coconut to copra

PRESERVING THE PAST IN THE PRESENT

★★★ **Fond Latisab Creole Park** (Sun–Fri, tours by appointment; tel: 450 5461) is a few miles south east of Babonneau via narrow country lanes in the small farming community of Fond Assau. The 4-hectare (11-acre) working farm, which cultivates nutmeg, cocoa and cinnamon and produces its own honey, lies between the Marquis and Louvet estates.

Fond Latisab maintains many aspects of traditional St Lucian culture, some of which stem back to when Amerindians inhabited the land, and practises farm techniques that have been passed on from father to son. For example, local guides are summoned by drumbeat. Even though there is a phone on the farm, much communication is done using the ancient art of drumming.

Visitors can watch log sawing done to the beating of drums accompanied by a *chak chak* band (named after the sound made by a local instrument). Log sawing by traditional method requires two men with skill rather than brute force to work the 3kg (6lb) tool. While sawing, the men sing Kwéyòl folk songs, accompanied by the band and the drum beats, which help to maintain rhythm. You can also see local people crayfishing, using traditional bamboo pots *(see page 46)*, and making cassava bread and farine – a flour produced from the root vegetable grown on the estate. Cassava bread is on sale when there is a tour, and home-grown nutmeg and cinnamon can also be purchased.

A FAR EASTERN DETOUR

Down the road from Fond Latisab, in Chassin, at the foot of La Sorcière hill, is the popular ★★★ **Rain Forest Adventures** (Dec–May Tue–Sun; entrance fee; tel: 458 5151; www.rainforest adventure.com). During a 2-hour tour, visitors are transported high above the forest in an aerial tram, which provides a bird's eye view of the landscape. Each gondola carries eight seated people and a guide to point out the different plants and trees as you glide through the forest canopy. After the ride you can buckle up to zip line through the forest, an adrenaline rush which is hugely enjoyable and great fun, with only basic levels of fitness and health required. The guides will jolly you along through any fears, but you can rest assured that safety standards are high even if they are unobtrusive. This is a popular excursion with cruise ship visitors so booking is essential. You can also take a guided nature walk. The Jacquot Trail up Mount La Sorcière starts from here, and guides are available for birdwatching hikes up the mountain at sunrise to try to spot the St Lucia parrot, which few visitors see in the wild.

Northwest of Babonneau, the winding Allan Bousquet Highway follows the Choc River, eventually leading to the ★ **Union Nature Trail** (daily 9am–4pm; no guided tours at the weekend; entrance fee) on an outpost of the Forestry and Lands Department. The trail loop begins on a path near the ranger station and can be covered in about an hour. It is a short walk (1.6km/1 mile) through dry forest with a few small hills, and can be enjoyed by any relatively fit visitor.

The collection of wildlife on the property is small, but includes native species such as agouti, iguana and the St Lucia parrot. There is also a herb garden growing plants with medicinal properties, that are used as traditional cures.

Back in Babonneau head northeast, this time to enjoy a landscape of sweeping valleys divided by rivers. The **Marquis Estate** sits in one such valley

Star Attractions
● **Fond Latisab Creole Park**
● **Rain Forest Adventures**
● **Union Nature Trail**

Creole culture
Fond Latisab Creole Park is part of a network of sites across the island that are members of the St Lucia Heritage Tourism Programme, which aims to encourage local communities to preserve and develop environmentally sensitive and sustainable tourist attractions.

Nutmeg and mace

Map on pages 34–5

with stands of teak, coffee and cocoa. The fertile soil and water supply from the Marquis River made the plantation an 18th-century success story for its French owners. The estate, which extends east to the coast, is to be developed as a five-star tourist resort with villas, golf course, marina, restaurants, equestrian centre, football academy, tennis academy and other luxury facilities. In the meantime it is closed to visitors.

TURTLE WATCHING

East of Desbarra stretches the beautiful beach at ★ ★ ★ **Grande Anse**, best known as a seasonal nesting site for the endangered leatherback turtle *(Demochelys coriacea)*. The valley in which this bay sits is thought to have historical significance because of the archaeological artefacts that have been discovered here, such as Amerindian petroglyphs, pottery shards and tools. The beach at Grande Anse, which along with the area's mangroves is part of a marine reserve, is best approached from Castries and the west on the highway to Babonneau, and then southeast on a minor road to the village of Desbarra perched on top of a mountain. The paved road stops here and a 4WD is essential unless you want a very long walk downhill. The beach can be seen in the distance just after the track passes the football field.

The leatherback (Demochelys coriacea) *is the world's largest turtle*

When you reach the bay you will find a rocky landscape and a secluded 2km (1.2-mile) strip of sand, which has reportedly been the target of illegal sand-miners. During the nesting season there have also been attempts to take valuable nesting turtles and their eggs. The sea around the bay is rough and strong winds can whip up the water, so it isn't safe to swim here, but a walk along the shore is a reward in itself.

From March to August the beach is monitored by the **Desbarra Grande Anse Turtle Watch Programme** *(see page 47)*, a community group that works in conjunction with the Ministry of Agriculture, Forestry and Fisheries. There are organised guided patrols of the beach to monitor the turtles and their nests during the nesting season. The group is also involved in education and conservation projects on the island.

According to a report by the Ministry, several other species of marine turtle, including the hawksbill turtle and the green turtle, travel long distances to the protected bay here and elsewhere in St Lucia.

Sea turtles will only leave the water to dig deep in the sand to lay their eggs; once that task is complete they return to the ocean. This is a crucial time, when the nests and eggs must remain undisturbed for around 60 days to allow the young to hatch. In an attempt to protect the endangered turtle population, it is prohibited to touch the eggs, hatchlings or a nesting turtle.

GRANDE ANSE ESTATE

The beach lies at the edge of the Grande Anse Estate, formerly a vast plantation spanning 810 hectares (2,000 acres). Today, much of the estate lands are uncultivated with cacti and dry forest peppering the hills and cliffs, providing a habitat for rare birds that include the St Lucia wren, the St Lucia oriole and the white-breasted thrasher. Snakes, such as the poisonous fer-de-lance and boa constrictor, and the protected iguana also form part of the estate's endemic wildlife. The Estate is also slated for development as a tourist resort.

Star Attraction
● Grande Anse

Turtle watch
The turtle watch patrols on Grande Anse beach begin in the early evening and continue until the following morning. The tours, which are part of the St Lucia Heritage Tourism Programme (HERITAS; tel: 458 1454; www.heritagetoursstlucia.org), are led by guides from the local community and welcome visitors from home and abroad. The tour includes transport from the hotel, to and from the beach, breakfast and dinner.

Sea turtles nest and lay their eggs on St Lucia's east coast beaches

Map on pages 34–5

Hardwood forest
Southwest of Anse La Raye is a large forest area that forms part of the Anse Galet Estate. This hardwood forest includes stands of tall evergreens.

3: Marigot Bay and Roseau Valley

Castries – Cul de Sac Valley – La Croix – Roseau Valley – Marigot Bay – Jacmel – Anse La Raye

Leaving downtown Castries behind, travellers heading south will discover the verdant St Lucian countryside opens up with wide expanses of farmland bordered by dense forest and laced by rivers. The Millennium Highway leads south out of Castries and towards the West Coast Road; it's a well-made road, relatively smooth but winding in places. As the road climbs up into the hills that signal the outskirts of the capital, you can look back at the view of Morne Fortune and Castries below.

Within minutes, the beginning of the semi-industrial area of the **Cul de Sac Valley** appears. At the side of the highway is a green space known as the Millennium Park, used as an open-air venue for a variety of festivities including New Year celebrations. In the bay beyond the park is a natural deep harbour and a vast terminal and storage facility for Hess Oil. Trees and farms border the road to the left, carpeting the land with fields of banana trees and other crops, while the Cul de Sac River cuts a path from the dense forested interior, meandering west to **Grande Cul de Sac Bay** where it flows into the Caribbean Sea.

Inspecting a banana plantation in the Cul de Sac Valley

ROSEAU VALLEY

At the end of the Millennium Highway the West Coast Road starts to climb past the Lucelec power station, which provides the main electricity supply to the greater part of the island. A little further on is the small village of La Croix on the edge of the rainforest. From this village, plantation land stretches away into the distance – this is the ★★**Roseau Valley**. The sprawling Roseau Plantation once extended over both the Roseau and the Cul de Sac valleys.

At the heart of the plantation area is the small village of **Roseau** which stands near farmland once owned by Geest before it was broken up and taken over by individual farmers. Today many of the farms form part of an agricultural collective providing bananas for European supermarkets *(see page 15)*. This is one of St Lucia's main banana producing regions and contains the largest banana plantation on the island.

Star Attractions
● **Roseau Valley**
● **Marigot Bay**

A PICTURESQUE HARBOUR

Before continuing south towards another of Roseau's attractions, consider taking a detour. Travel in a northerly direction for less than 1km (⅔ mile) for spectacular views over the surrounding hills and picturesque harbour. The road climbs northwest through the valley and at the next left turn the route climbs up a steep hill before descending to ★ ★ ★ **Marigot Bay**. During the day the bay feels a little isolated and away from it all, despite being only 5km (3 miles) from Castries centre, but that's part of its enduring attraction.

Below: western St Lucia is farming and fishing country
Bottom: Marigot Bay

There is a small palm-fringed beach and a sheltered natural harbour, which includes The Moorings, a yacht and sailing base and equipment facility, making the bay a popular choice among local sailors and visitors who spend the winter in the Caribbean. On the south side of the bay is the Discovery resort; above it palatial homes and villas pepper the hillside landscape, some of which are available for rent *(see page 116)*.

Map on pages 34–5

NORTH SIDE OF THE BAY

The north side of the bay is accessible only by boat, but that small detail doesn't appear to put people off: Marigot Bay is well known for its lively nightlife and the north side is dotted with a healthy number of bars and restaurants. As the evening descends the traffic across the bay increases with boats sailing to-and-fro. An inexpensive and regular ferry (water taxi) service operates 24 hours per day. The water around the bay where the Marigot Beach Club Hotel and Dive Resort (tel: 451 4974) is located is ideal for swimming and the resort also fronts the area's best beach. Visitors are drawn to the place primarily because of its pretty location but also for its restaurant, Doolittle's, named after the film that was shot here in the 1960s.

Below: rum, the spirit of St Lucia
Bottom: on the beach at Marigot Bay

But it's not all flashy resorts and alfresco dining around the bay. The eastern part of the lagoon has a small mangrove swamp, a natural site that has been protected with reserve status.

Nearby St Lucian-owned and operated JJ's Paradise Resort has a boardwalk that meanders through the mangroves and joins the back of the property to the dockside.

SUGAR CANE

Before bananas, sugar was the agricultural mainstay and it is this crop that transformed the lush

river valleys in the 18th century. The demand for sugar and its by-products, especially rum, from Europe and further afield prompted St Lucian farmers to import enslaved men and women from West Africa to carry out the back-breaking work on the land until slavery was abolished in the 19th century.

Successful for a time, St Lucia was forced to diversify in the mid-20th century following the introduction to Europe of cheaper sugar produced from sugar beet and fierce competition from high-volume sugar producers elsewhere in the Caribbean. The Roseau sugar refinery struggled on but eventually it too gave up; it was one of the last sugar factories to close in 1963.

Star Attraction
● St Lucia Distillers

Talk to the animals
Marigot Bay was immortalised on the silver screen when it was used as a location for the Hollywood film, *Dr Dolittle*, in 1967. Rex Harrison starred in the movie.

A RUM BUSINESS

Cane sugar production fuelled the rum industry on the island but by the 1970s sugar cane was no longer being grown here. The Barnard family estate, which operated a distillery in Dennery, entered into a joint venture with Geest and moved to the Roseau Valley. Molasses, the raw material for rum production, are now shipped in from Guyana and today the ★★**St Lucia Distillers** (Mon–Fri 9am–3pm; entrance fee; reservations essential 24 hrs in advance, call for tour times; tel: 456 3148; www.saintluciarums.com) produces a wide selection of rums and liqueurs. Among the dark rums, look for the award-winning Admiral Rodney, an aged rum which should be drunk neat, or the Chairman's Reserve, also good on the rocks. Bounty is the dark rum you will see most commonly on the island, while Crystal is the white rum used in cocktails (*see page 96*).

The distillery is signposted from the West Coast Road. Travelling from north to south, pass the Marigot Bay turn and Marigot school, and continue until you reach a junction. Take a right along a rough, pot-holed access road (muddy in the rain). At the end is the rum factory, with a visitors' centre, a shop and a warehouse. This was also the site of a 19th-century, steam-

Everything you need for a day at Marigot Bay

Map on pages 34–5

Map on pages 34–5

West Coast wind down
The fish fry at Anse La Raye is popular with tourists and locals alike. People come to unwind at the end of the week and lobster is a speciality when in season.

Fishing boats at Anse La Raye

powered sugar mill, with a narrow-gauge railway and steam engine used to transport the cane and molasses. The distillery organises lively guided tours, which reveal how rum was made in the past and how it is produced today. The tour ends with a rum buffet where you can try the 20 or so products they make, from sweet flavoured rums (peanut, coconut, cocoa) to the Denros 160° proof firewater, which eases aching joints if rubbed on them.

The small hill community of **Jacmel**, which lies east of the Roseau Valley, has a church with a striking painting of a black Madonna and child and other St Lucian figures by the artist Dunstan St Omer. It is best visited with a local guide, as even in daylight the winding, narrow roads are difficult to negotiate.

ANSE LA RAYE

The West Coast Road carves a direct route south through the plateau of the Roseau Valley, its banana plantations and the surrounding rolling hills to Soufrière. The road links small rural villages and as you near the coast the farming communities that produce bananas and cassava give way to sleepy fishing hamlets.

The journey weaves through the historically important village of Massacré and descends to sleepy ★★**Anse La Raye**. At first glance there isn't much to recommend the village; its narrow streets are lined with nondescript small shops and residences. But at the entrance to the village a sign points the way towards the small **Anse La Raye waterfall**, reachable with the help of a local guide by a short walk through the undergrowth. Sadly, no swimming is allowed at these falls.

The village itself has a police station, a community centre, a Catholic church and a filling station, while along the sea front small, brightly painted fishing boats bob in the water and fishermen's huts on the beach provide shelter and shade for repairing a seine (net). The pace is relaxed and as people go about their business visitors can get a sense of the real St Lucia without the tourist gloss.

FRIDAY FISH FRY

Friday evening is a different story altogether, for this is when the village wakes up and comes alive with a Friday fish fry. The event is almost a precursor to the Gros Islet Jump-up on the northwest coast *(see page 40)*, but Anse La Raye's is a much more relaxed affair with families coming along. In the early evening the road is blocked off as stallholders set up coal pots and barbecues in front of the fishermen's huts and lay out tables so that people can enjoy their meal in the open air while they soak up the atmosphere. By 9pm the place is packed and loud music punctuates the air while locals and visitors alike walk the length of the road to see what's on offer before making a choice from a variety of dishes. On sale are fish most likely caught that day, such as red snapper, kingfish and dolphin (dorado or mahi-mahi), and lobster when in season, along with potfish, conch salad, breadfruit salad and floats and bakes (similar to fried dumplings), washed down with a Piton beer or soft drink. The village bars are also busy with the usual end-of-the-week crowd swelled by people at the fish fry. Some very basic public facilities are available near the fishermen's huts.

Star Attraction
● Anse La Raye

Below: Anse La Raye
Bottom: the art of Dunstan St Omer in Jacmel church

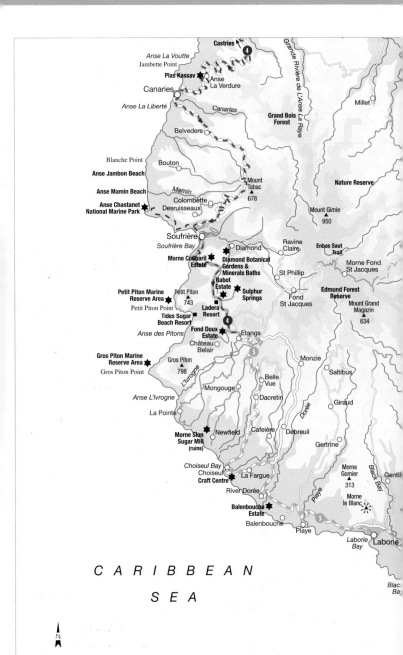

Cul de Sac

BARRE DE L'ISLE RIDGE

Grande Rivière du Mabouya

Grand Rivière, Castries

Fond D'Or Bay

Dennery

La Croix Point

Dennery

Dennery Island
Dennery Bay

Errard Estate

Linnis Point

Mamiku

**Fregate Islands
Nature Reserve**

Praslin

Praslin Island

**Mamiku
Gardens**
Mamiku

*Praslin
Bay*

Martelly Point

Trou Gras Point

Mon
Repos

Anse Patience

Patience

Fond

Anse Chapeau

Malgrétoute

Anse Violon

Violon Point

Mahaut

Fond Bay

**Quiesse
Forest
Reserve**

Rain Forest Walk

**Latille
Waterfall**

Troumassée

Ti Rocher

Micoud

Carelles

Vierge Point

Blanchard

Troumassé Bay

Desruisseaux

A T L A N T I C

Belle Vue

O C E A N

Grande Rivière du Vieux Fort

Anse Ger

Pierrot

Pointe Lamarre

Petite Rivière du Vieux Fort

Augier

St Urbain

Savannes Bay Nature Reserve

Pointe de Caille

Scorpion I.
*Savannes
Bay*

**Mankoté
Mangrove**

Mill (Ruins)

Derrière
Morne

**Hewanorra
International Airport**

Point Sable

Georgie
Point

Vieux Fort

**Maria Islands
Nature Reserve**

*Vieux Fort
Bay*

*Anse de
Sables*

--- 5 --- **Described routes**

Caesar Point

Cap Moule à Chique

ROUTES 4-6

0   2 km

0   2 miles

Ministre Point

Dennery

Mamiku

Map
on pages
34–5 &
58–9

4: Soufrière and the West Coast

Anse La Raye – Canaries – Soufrière – Anse Chastanet – Diamond Botanical Gardens – La Soufrière Sulphur Springs – Petit Piton – Gros Piton

The journey south to Soufrière, along the West Coast, goes from urban to countryside almost immediately. Though tiny, even by Caribbean standards, the island encompasses a wide variety of landscapes from open plains to rolling hills and valleys, ragged mountain ranges and lush rainforest. The West Coast Road is well made and the stretch from the capital through the Roseau Valley is fairly easy to negotiate. As the road descends to Anse La Raye and beyond, its twists and turns requiring skilful and careful driving. Repairs were still ongoing in 2011 following landslips after Hurricane Tomas. In places you can see that the road has been literally cut through the hills and is shaded by mature trees and vegetation, while farms and fishing villages dot the panorama below.

Cassava bread
If you want to take some cassava bread home, the best way to preserve it is to freeze it. Buy the bread as close to your departure date as possible, but leave enough time for it to freeze solid. Once frozen, wrap it up well and transport it in a cool bag. Eat within a day of defrosting.

LA SIKWI'S SWEET HISTORY

On the outskirts of Anse La Raye a path leads to a restored sugar mill south of the village, just before the bridge that stretches across the Grande Rivière de L'Anse La Raye. ★ **La Sikwi Sugar Mill** (entrance fee; tel: 451 4245) was constructed by the British in 1876 on the original Invergoil Estate. The mill, which once ground sugar cane to make molasses, but was later converted for lime oil production, has a small museum and is used as a lunch stop by cruise ship tour parties.

The current estate owners have tried to keep a naturalness about the land; shady trails circle the lush gardens full of bright blooms and a cooling 15m (50ft) waterfall is a popular spot with local children, who also play by the nearby river. Although the mill is no longer operational, it is in good condition with a large wheel and other components and conveys a sense of the backbreaking and monotonous life of slaves and farm labourers.

Cassava is a St Lucian staple

A St Lucian Speciality

On the route south the road winds sharply as it cuts its way through the undulating hills down to the valley. In places there are stunning views of the coast and the Pitons – Gros Piton and Petit Piton – as the road skirts along the cliffs with a sheer drop to dense vegetation below. Where the road widens, the homes of local people are set back slightly, then in a curve in the road, opposite a stand of trees at Anse La Verdure, is ★ **Plas Kassav** (daily 8.30am–7 or 8pm; tel: 459 4050; www.plaskassav.com).

Star Attractions
- **La Sikwi Sugar Mill**
- **Plas Kassav**

This family bakery uses traditional methods and some innovative equipment to produce farine (from cassava) and a mouth-watering variety of cassava bread that is popular with local workers, especially at lunchtime. Several cruise ships and organised tours make this a regular stop, providing people with an opportunity to taste one of the island's specialities, and you can buy some to take back home.

Below: hill country
Bottom: children in a fishing village on the west coast

Attached to the bakery is a small shop that sells refreshments and cassava bread in a choice of flavours including coconut, peanut butter, cherry and raisin, cinnamon, salt, saltfish and smoked herring. The bread makes a hearty snack or can be used as an accompaniment to a meal. Other local products such as dried bananas, pepper sauces and honey are also sold in the shop.

Map
on pages
58–9

FISHING AND FOREST

A few minutes drive from Anse La Verdure is **Canaries** (pronounced can-ar-ees), a small village where most families eke out a living from the fruits of the sea. There is some discussion about where the village's name originates – is it from seafarers who originally hailed from the Canary Islands or named after an Amerindian pot (called a *kannawi*) used by the people who settled here? Archaeological discoveries nearby support the latter theory.

The **Canaries River** flows through the forest and out to sea here, supporting a handful of waterfalls to the south of the village. Most are hard to find without a guide and require a 30-minute hike, at the very least, to reach them.

Only a few minutes south of Canaries, off the West Coast Road is a nature site that was formerly the Anse La Liberté campsite. Currently there is no official place to camp on the island. The land, which is managed by the St Lucia National Trust, extends 56 hectares (138 acres) into the forest. It has around 6km (4 miles) of walking trails, a good beach and some basic visitor facilities. You can also reach it by water taxi from Canaries.

GRAND BOIS FOREST

The Pitons

Inland and east of Canaries, near Belvedere, is **Grand Bois Forest**. Views of the cool and shady

vegetation can be seen from the winding road and the forest is the habitat of several endemic plant species and wildlife, with mature stands of bamboo, palms and tropical fern.

As the road snakes through the hills you can enjoy stunning views of the sea and the spectacular western landscape backed by the magnificent Pitons, which dominate the area, lying just beyond the centre of Soufrière. Before that, **Mount Tabac** comes into view, rising high above the hills and forests to its 678m (2,224ft) peak.

Before the road begins its descent to the next town is **Colombette**, one of the villages worst hit by Hurricane Tomas in 2010 in terms of loss of life. Sabinus 'Sabby' Thomas and his wife were killed when a mudslide wiped out their home and their Livity Craft Studio. Sabby was well known in the arts and crafts world and was part of a local cooperative, exhibiting his white cedar chairs, calabash bowls and basketwork at many craft fairs.

> **Bay of Freedom**
> The bay of Anse La Liberté, south of Canaries, is thought to have historical significance. It is believed that enslaved African men and women living and working on the island celebrated their emancipation here in 1834, hence the name – Anse La Liberté (Bay of Freedom).

SOUFRIÈRE

The rural west is an antidote to the hustle and bustle of the capital; life moves at a much slower pace here. The journey from Castries to Soufrière takes about an hour and a quarter, even though the distance between the two places is only about 32km (20 miles). The road along the West Coast, heading north to south, is winding, with sharp bends in places once you leave the Millennium Highway just outside Castries. You must have your wits about you if you intend to drive yourself because these mountain roads can be unforgiving, with steep drops down to the valley below. In 2011 there were still ongoing repairs after the 2010 hurricane, and heavy rain frequently brought more mud onto the road.

To the east is **Mount Gimie**, which at more than 950m (3,145ft) high stands above both of the better-known peaks of the Pitons (see page 75). The road twists, rises and falls towards the sea and the heart of the West Coast, surrounded by mountains and dense protected forests and

Map
on page
63

lapped by clear waters that shelter spectacular dive sites. Several viewpoints are marked along the West Coast Road where you can stop to look down over the picturesque bay, especially pretty if there is a tall ship in the harbour.

ST LUCIA'S OLDEST TOWN

Established in the 18th century, ★★**Soufrière** is St Lucia's oldest town and was the capital when France controlled the island. It stands in the shadow of the island's most striking and best-known landmark – the twin peaks of the Pitons rising majestically out of the sea. Louis XIV of France granted around 809 hectares (2,000 acres) of land to the Devaux family, who ran a successful plantation growing sugar, cocoa, tobacco and cotton on the estate. Descendants of the family still own land and property in the area today. For many years after the country was ceded to the British, Soufrière remained little more than a small fishing village, but today it is expanding. The population of the village proper and its environs is now believed to be close to 8,000.

Impressive tall ships
The Brig *Unicorn* was built in 1946 and is a replica of a ship from 1850. The brig has masts 30m (100ft) tall carrying 600 sq m (6,500 sq ft) of sail needing 5km (3 miles) of rope. While it is out of service you will still see a tall ship bringing pirate tours to Soufrière from the north of the island. The Nova Scotia tall ship, *Liana's Ransom*, is a 25m (85ft), gaff-rigged, square topsail schooner, from which you can swing from the yard arm or walk the plank.

SOUFRIÈRE'S LAYOUT

Enter the village via a small bridge over the **Soufrière River**, which flows to the sea just to the west. On the left is a Shell petrol station (cash only), to the right is the town hall and after that, business and residential properties line both sides of Bridge Street, the main road. Heading south turn right into Sir Darnley Alexander Street and then left into Maurice Mason Street (also known as Bay Street) to reach the waterfront. Facing the small harbour is the police station and the post office. A gift shop, which sells souvenirs and items made by local artists, is on the town square.

Seine, sea and Piton

COLONIAL ARCHITECTURE

Modern and colonial buildings stand side by side; painted in pastels, many have pretty balconies with gingerbread fretwork. Most notable is the

Old Courthouse at the southern end of the waterfront. Constructed in 1898, the historic stone, colonial-style building has been a restaurant but is now closed.

The waterfront has a small paved area with seats looking out across the harbour, which is often dominated by the large sail-assisted cruise ships that frequent the port for a few hours. The deep harbour drops to 60m (200ft) close to shore so Windjammer yachts and sailing ships can dock right at the pier, while the larger Star Clippers drop anchor just outside and tender passengers to dry land. A common sight here is the *Liana's Ransom*, which regularly brings passengers on day trips from Castries (*see box left, and page 29*).

SOUFRIÈRE MARINE MANAGEMENT AREA

At the northern end of the pier is another jetty, the **Soufrière Marine Management Area** (SMMA) office, a water taxi station and tour office where you can book transport around the coast. Visitors can go to places that are difficult to reach by road, and also to some of the island's best dive sites, as well as join boat trips around the Pitons.

The SMMA, which extends from Anse Jambon to Anse L'Ivrogne almost at the foot of Gros Piton, was established in 1994 to protect the unique marine habitat along the west coast of St

Star Attraction
● Soufrière

A pretty Soufrière balcony and boats in the busy harbour

Map on page 63

Lucia. It regularly monitors the coral reefs and water quality, carrying out scientific research in an attempt to prevent damage to reefs, fish stock, beaches and vegetation as Soufrière and its environs along the west coast continue to develop.

Its four main protected Marine Reserve Areas (MRAs), for which you will require a permit to dive, are:

• Anse Chastanet
• Rachette Pointe
• Petit Piton
• Gros Piton (restricted access)

Permits can be purchased on an annual or daily basis and are available from the SMMA (tel: 459 5500) and authorised dive operators.

EXPLORING SOUFRIÈRE

Soufrière can be easily explored on foot; there are few sights, and most are within a few minutes' walk of the water. Most of the area's attractions are either on, or underneath the water, or in and around the rainforest. What the town does have is atmosphere. A handful of vendors sell local produce from the street around the corner from the tourist office, and on Saturday there is a busy street market near the waterfront for early risers.

The airy **Lady of Assumption Church**, built in the 1950s, stands at the corners of Henry Belmar, Sir Arthur Lewis and Boulevard streets. It has a simple design with the lovely altar and pulpit made from dark tropical wood. Above the main doors is a magnificent pipe organ.

Children in the town square with the Lady of Assumption in the background

TOWN SQUARE HUSTLERS

Just in front of the church steps is the **town square** where a guillotine was erected by the Brigands *(see pages 32–3)* during the French Revolution. If you wander through the small square be aware that this is one place where there is relatively high unemployment. You may be solicited for money or be approached by an unofficial (and unwanted) guide offering to show you around the church; a guide is not necessary, so a firm but polite refusal should suffice. If you do want a guide to show you around town, ask the staff at your hotel to recommend a reliable one. On the north side of the square, on Henry Belmar Street, you will find buses for Castries and on the south side, on Sir Arthur Lewis Street, are buses for Vieux Fort and the south.

DIVING DELIGHT

★★★ **Anse Chastanet** is a national marine park and well-known dive area just north of Soufrière, but the access road is potholed and narrow so you would be best advised to take a water taxi around the bay. To reach the beach from Soufrière by road, travel back as if returning to Castries, but as you cross the bridge on the edge of town veer left. It's a tortuous but rewarding 15-minute journey.

The Anse Chastanet Resort dominates the beaches and 243 hectares (600 acres) of verdant land here. Spacious and luxurious tree-house style, open-air rooms built in to the hillside look out to the Pitons, and a dive operation, **Scuba St Lucia**, rents snorkelling and scuba-diving equipment. PADI and NAUI scuba courses are available for everyone, from beginners to the more experienced.

Volcanic black sand fronts the hotel, while the ★★ **Anse Chastanet reef**, with a host of colour-

Star Attraction
● Anse Chastanet

Protect the reefs
● Do not damage or touch the coral while you are snorkelling or diving.
● Do not remove any plants, animals, fish or even shells from the sea.
● Do not feed the fish.
● Tie up only to mooring buoys or anchor at official sandy areas.
● Do not buy souvenirs made from coral; it is illegal to remove it from St Lucia.
● Do not buy souvenirs or other items made from turtle shells.
● Do not litter; dispose of waste in the appropriate bins.

Soufrière has colourful marine life, ideal for diving

Map on pages 58–9

Driving
Drive at your own pace and allow local drivers to pass you as you take your time and reach your destination safely. It's best to opt for an automatic hire car, which will help when driving along the narrow twisting mountain roads. If you want to drive in the deep rural areas where the roads are steep and more than often poorly maintained, be sure to rent a four-wheel drive.

Diamond Botanical Gardens

ful marine life, offers the opportunity to walk to a dive site within a few metres of the shore, where there are bright displays of coral, sponges, angelfish, parrot fish and seahorses. North of Anse Chastanet are two fine golden sand beaches, ★★ **Anse Mamin** and ★★ **Anse Jambon**. Anse Mamin is ideal for a picnic or a day spent relaxing on the beach and its clear waters. The beach is backed by forest and former plantation land from where **Bike St Lucia** (tel: 459 2453; www.bikestlucia.com) organises energetic cycling trips, known as jungle biking, along 19km (12 miles) of bike trails through the 18th-century plantation.

MINERAL BATHS AND FLOWERS

South of Soufrière, old estate houses and hotels populate the hillsides, mostly shielded from the road by magnificent trees and bordered by fertile farmland. Head east out of town on Sir Arthur Lewis Street and a few kilometres along a good road you will reach the ★★★ **Diamond Botanical Gardens**, **Mineral Baths and Waterfall** (Mon–Sat 10am–5pm, Sun and public hols 10am–3pm; entrance fee; tel: 459 7565; www.diamondstlucia.com). The gardens were originally part of the Soufrière Estate, awarded to the Devaux family *(see page 64)* in the early 18th century by King Louis XIV of France. The original baths were built in 1784 by the Governor of St Lucia, Baron de Laborie, after it was discovered that water from the sulphur springs was mineral rich and therefore an effective treatment for rheumatism and other ailments. The baths were financed by King Louis XVI for his troops on the island, but they were destroyed during battles with the Brigands *(see page 32)* around the time of the French Revolution. The bathing pools were restored in 1925, while the garden and other facilities were expanded later to provide bathing in a communal outdoor pool or individual baths, for an additional fee. Beyond the baths is the waterfall, and there is a small shop with reasonably priced souvenirs and snacks.

A short trail snakes through the gardens and

useful and descriptive signs identify tropical flora such as fragrant frangipani, red ginger, vibrant hibiscus and a variety of trees laden with coconut, cocoa or other local staples, so a guide is not necessary. A longer and more strenuous hike, which crosses over the **Diamond River**, leads to the old mill and a working waterwheel.

Star Attractions
● Anse Mamin
● Anse Jambon
● Diamond Botanical Gardens
● Morne Coubaril

PLANTATION LIFE

★★ **Morne Coubaril Estate** (daily 9am–4pm; entrance fee; guided tours; tel: 459 7340; email: coubaril@candw.lc) lies less than 1km (⅔ mile) from Soufrière on the Soufrière–Vieux Fort Road, almost opposite the slip road leading to the Jalousie Plantation resort.

Below: colourful orchids
Bottom: the beach at Anse Chastanet

The 113-hectare (280-acre) working plantation is one of the oldest on the island. It was owned by the Devaux family until 1960 when it was taken over by Donald Monplaisir. The Monplaisir family have attempted to restore and preserve the property and it's agricultural traditions. Although the great house is not open to the public because it remains a family home, visitors can view the exterior of the building, which is in excellent condition with lovely wrap-around verandas.

Colourful flora and trees heavy with fruit such as papaya, banana, coconut, orange and grapefruit grow in abundance. There are also cocoa

Map on pages 58–9

trees and if you are lucky you may get the chance to taste the sweet pulp that surrounds the seeds inside the cocoa pod.

WALKS AND TALKS

Fascinating walking tours of the property take in the Copra House, where coconuts are prepared for sale to the St Lucia Coconut Growers Association, which produces coconut oil, and there is a lovely view over the deep bay nearby. You can also see a fully operational sugar mill where a mule is used to turn the wheel that grinds the sugar cane and produces the juice to make sugar and rum.

Plantation work was back-breaking and the enslaved Africans and farm labourers endured a hard life. Replica wooden slave quarters reveal how people were forced to live in basic and cramped conditions. The huts have been reconstructed using traditional methods, with mud and paper on the walls and palm thatch on the roof.

Morne Coubaril also organises trekking expeditions on horseback (by appointment) and a choice of rainforest hikes (up to 3 hours) that visit the **Coubaril waterfall**, which is fed by the Sulphur Springs. Though strenuous, the walks are fun with an informative guide and reach a lookout point that provides a panoramic view over Soufrière.

Below: hiking with a guide
Bottom: Diamond Botanical Gardens

'DRIVE-IN' VOLCANO

Beyond Morne Coubaril plantation, off the Soufrière–Vieux Fort Road are ★★ **La Soufrière Sulphur Springs** (daily 9am–5pm; entrance fee), notable for the pungent odour (hydrogen sulphide), not dissimilar to rotten eggs. At times, when a strong wind blows and the vapours are high, the whiff can be detected at quite a distance. As a result of hurricane damage, the entrance was blocked in 2011 and alternative access was being used (turn east by the Rabot Estate, opposite Ladera Resort).

La Soufrière volcano collapsed more than 40,000 years ago and now produces only the foul-smelling gases and hot water that can reach temperatures of 170°C (338°F). At the ticket booth, be prepared for vendors who congregate here to offer their wares; official guides also wait to escort visitors, for an additional fee, down a wooden pathway and along some uneven ground. He or she will give you a rundown of the site and its history.

The rocky landscape of the geothermal field looks like something from a science-fiction movie, with springs and grey-brown mud bubbling up sporadically. In 2011 it was also littered with trees and debris brought down by the hurricane. Be careful when you are on the walkway as the bubbling mud and water is scalding.

CHOCOLATE HEAVEN

At the turn off for the volcano is the entrance for the ★★ **Rabot Estate** (tel: 457 1624; www.thehotel chocolat.com), a recently rehabilitated 56-hectare (140-acre) cocoa plantation owned by the British chocolatiers, Hotel Chocolat. The plantation dates back to 1745 and is the oldest on the island, with some very rare old trees of scientific and chocolate interest. This is a true bean-to-bar experience, as they grow their own cocoa before making it into their own delicious St Lucia chocolate. The chocolate-making is performed in the UK, but a factory is being built here so that the entire process will soon be carried out on the island, creating lots of new jobs. Local cocoa farmers also benefit as

Star Attractions
● Sulphur Springs
● Rabot Estate

Scientific research
The Sulphur Springs are believed to be the hottest geothermal area in the Lesser Antilles. Scientists have carried out a variety of research at the springs, such as its potential as a geothermal energy source. They have recorded temperatures of more than 170°C (338°F) from fumaroles (steam vents).

A colourful country cottage on Morne Coubaril Estate

Map on pages 58–9

Battle of Rabot

The Fond Doux Estate is close to the site of the Battle of Rabot, fought in 1795, when freedom fighters forced the British military to retreat outside Soufrière. The previous year, the new French Republic had granted freedom to enslaved Africans in its foreign territories. But when St Lucia was again brought under British influence the emancipated islanders feared they would be returned to bondage, hence the resulting rebellion.

Drying cocoa beans at the Fond Doux Estate

the estate buys their quality cacao pods at premium prices and guarantees a market for their product while also supplying them with young trees to improve their stock.

In 2011, a hotel was opened on the estate with luxury cottages and villas in view of the Pitons, together with the Boucan restaurant which specializes in all things chocolate, both savoury and sweet *(see page 98)*. You can walk to the site of the Battle of Rabot, stroll through the plantation tasting the fruits of the mango, guava, soursop and papaya trees, then relax with a cocoa massage using the cacao nibs, oil and butter.

FOND DOUX ESTATE

South of Rabot Estate is the ★★**Fond Doux Estate** (daily 8am–4pm for tours, until 10pm for dinner; entrance fee; tel: 459 7545; www.fonddoux estate.com), a working plantation. An inexpensive guided tour includes a look at the original plantation house, built in 1864 and renovated in the 1990s, which is currently occupied. Adjacent to the estate house is a colonial-style restaurant, which serves a buffet lunch for tour groups, a bar and a souvenir shop. The grounds, which extend over 55 hectares (135 acres), are planted with coffee, banana, mango, citrus fruits and coconut. Surplus spices, fruit and vegetables are sold in the owners' supermarket in Soufrière. There is still an original worker's house, store house, copra house and coffee-drying area on the property, as well as cottages available to rent.

Cocoa grown here is shipped to the UK and to the United States for use in chocolate produced by the Hershey Food Corporation. The drying racks are still in operation and you will be shown how cocoa sticks are made. These are available to buy in the shop. A leisurely walk through the estate reveals an abundance of bright and fragrant flora such as heliconia, ginger lilies and anthuriums. Trails through the estate lead past ruined military buildings built by French engineers in the 18th century, while up on the hill is an old Brigands' hideout used during a battle against the British in 1795.

AMERINDIAN HERITAGE

The area around Soufrière has been an important settlement for centuries, long before the French or British arrived. The Amerindian settlers were in awe of the volcano, where the Island Arawaks thought their god, Yokahu, slept and the Caribs named it Qualibou, or the place of death. Archaeological evidence of their presence can still be found on the ground.

There are petroglyphs along paths on both the **Jalousie** and **Stonefield Estates**. The former Jalousie Plantation hotel was built amid a wave of controversy when local people, environmentalists and archaeologists objected to its location due to its proximity to the Pitons *(see page 75)*, now a World Heritage Site, and also because it was built on an important Amerindian burial ground, which is now under the tennis courts.

RAINFOREST MOUNTAIN RESERVES

Most of the mountainous heart of St Lucia has been declared forest reserve, partly to protect wildlife and partly to preserve water supply for the settlements around the coast of the island. In some areas there are trails through the forest, maintained by the Forestry Department (tours Mon–Fri 8.30am–3pm; entrance fee; tel: 468 5649 or 450 2231; http://malff.com; *see page 104)*,

Star Attraction
● **Fond Doux Estate**

La Soufrière Sulphur Springs

Map
on pages
58–9

Lord Glenconner

British entrepreneur and aristocrat, the late Colin Tennant (Lord Glenconner), who died in 2010, previously owned the Jalousie Estate, as well as the Grenadine island of Mustique, where he entertained Princess Margaret and her friends. For many years he ran a bar, Bang Between the Pitons, which was popular with celebrities and yachties, but which has now been subsumed by the resort hotel.

and it is possible to hike from west to east coasts starting from Soufrière.

A simple walk in the rainforest is a rewarding experience, preferably with a Forest Ranger to guide you. Six miles (10km) east of Soufrière lies the village of **Fond St Jacques**, where there are paintings by Dunstan St Omer in the church, used to shelter homeless families after Hurricane Tomas. This village suffered one of the worst mudslides and the gash is still visible on the mountainside. From the village, there is a poor road leading up to a Rangers' station. To reach it, either use a four-wheel drive vehicle or walk.

With advance notice, the rangers will escort you through the **Edmund Forest Reserve** to the **Quilesse Forest Reserve** and down to the Rangers' station on the **Des Cartiers Rainforest Trail**, near Mahaut and to Micoud on the east coast. Alternatively, for a shorter excursion, follow the ★★**Enbas Saut Trail** from the Rangers' station above Fond St Jacques. This steep but exhilarating trail winds down 2,112 steps cut in the hillside to the Troumassée River, providing an opportunity to see elfin woodland, cloud forest and rainforest, depending on your altitude. You will be able to see the peaks of Piton Canarie, Piton Troumassée and Morne Gimie and you will hear the St Lucian parrot in the trees above you. At the bottom there are a couple of river cross-

Ladera Resort overlooks the Pitons

ings before you reach a pool with a little water-fall, where you can cool off before the arduous hike back up. Expect to get wet and muddy, especially after rain, which is frequent.

SCALING THE PITONS

★★★ **The Pitons** dominate the southwestern landscape around Soufrière. **Petit Piton** (743m/2,438ft) is to the north of Soufrière harbour, while **Gros Piton** (798m/2,618ft) is on the south side of the bay near the L'Ivrogne River. The tall volcanic cones, which are covered in rich vegetation, are undoubtedly the most photographed rocks in St Lucia. A UNESCO World Heritage Site, their image appears on everything from postcards to T-shirts and art.

For many people the Pitons offer pleasure simply for their sheer beauty. However, more adventurous spirits want to get to the top. Though Petit Piton is the smaller of the two, it is more difficult to climb because of its steep sides, making climbing ropes essential. A relatively easier option is the trail up Gros Piton, although this isn't a walk in the park either. It is not a pursuit to be tackled alone and you will need to employ the services of a local guide. Contact the Soufrière Regional Development Foundation (tel: 459 5500), or the Gros Piton Guides Association (tel: 459 3492). Be prepared for a very early start – most guides recommend setting off and reaching your goal early in the morning before it gets too hot.

Scaling the peak can be hot and thirsty work, so remember to carry plenty of water, sunblock and a hat for shade. The time taken to complete the climb can vary; it is generally between three and six hours each way depending on the hiker's level of fitness. The hike begins along an uneven path at the wide base of the rock where you may be able to spot a rare bird, such as the St Lucian oriole, and other wildlife. Remember that you don't have to climb to the summit, but if you do you will be rewarded with sweeping panoramic views over the island, north and south, and on a clear day as far as neighbours Martinique and St Vincent.

Star Attractions
- **Enbas Saut Trail**
- **The Pitons**

The Tet Paul Trail
This is an easy alternative for those not fit enough to scale Gros Piton. This 45-minute walk begins in the Chateau Belair community in 2.4 hectares (6 acres) of lush vegetation between Fond Doux and the Gros Piton Trail. Head for Fond Doux and you will see the sign at the entrance to the Plantation. You walk through a variety of fruit trees and medicinal plants and can enjoy views of the Pitons, Jalousie beach, the coastline to the south and the neighbouring islands.

Follow a forest trail

Map
on pages
58–9

Second city
Vieux Fort is considered to be St Lucia's second city, with a developing industrial centre and a population of 15,000.

5: Vieux Fort and the South

Soufrière – Choiseul – Balenbouche – Vieux Fort – Cap Moule à Chique – Maria Islands Nature Reserve – Savannes Bay Nature Reserve

Although greatly improved, the road south from Soufrière to Vieux Fort, now known as the West Caribbean Coast Road, is still winding. It dips and rises through the hills and valleys, skirting forest and farmland, eventually passing through the small fishing hamlets that dot the southwestern coast. The road to and beyond Choiseul was difficult to negotiate for many years, but a major roadworks improvement programme has cut journey time. It now takes less than an hour to reach Vieux Fort.

KEEP ON MOVING

Leaving Soufrière and its environs you will pass by a good many attractions covered in Route 4 *(see page 60)* such as the Ladera Resort, Rabot Estate and the Fond Doux Estate before you reach Etangs on the Choiseul road.

The trip southwest provides visitors with the chance to see rural St Lucia up close, enjoying views of the Pitons, particularly **Gros Piton** which sits on the edge of the district known as the Quarter of Choiseul. On a clear day, you may also catch a glimpse of neighbouring St Vincent's volcanic mountain, called La Soufrière too.

UNTOUCHED LANDSCAPES

From Etangs the main road heads due south to Choiseul but you can take a detour along the L'Ivrogne river to the coast. The road turns through several small rural communities barely touched by tourism. On the coast road before you reach Newfield is a wide expanse of farmland that overlooks the sea, and nearby is a local landmark – the ruins of **Morne Sion Sugar Mill**, which used three windmills to crush its sugar cane, the only one of its kind on the island. Two windmills are in ruins but the third has been restored, although without its sails.

A country car wash in the Balenbouche River

A TOWN OF ARTISANS

Choiseul is a good-size town with a developed centre that has a town hall, a church, several schools, a post office and petrol station. The ruins of **Fort Citreon**, a fortress which protected Choiseul Bay, still stands guard over the area, but Choiseul is best known for ★★**La Fargue Craft Centre**. This is where local artisans sell their work, such as clay pots, for which the area is well known, basketwork, woodcarvings, local spices, seasonings and sauces. The centre is on the main drag and has plenty of parking space. The poor state of the roads in the past forced several artists to relocate to areas more accessible to visitors, but there are still craftsmen based around here and the centre can direct you to their workshops if you want something a bit different which is not in stock.

BALENBOUCHE ESTATE

A few miles down the road is the ★★**Balenbouche Estate** (daily; entrance fee; guided tours by appointment; tel: 455 1244; www.balenbouche.com), which stands proudly on 30 hectares (75 acres) between the Balenbouche and Piaye rivers. It is close to some important historical and archaeological sites, and nearby **Morne le Blanc** has a good lookout point.

Star Attractions
- **La Fargue Craft Centre**
- **Balenbouche Estate**

Balenbouche Estate house: exterior and interior views

Map on pages 58–9

GREAT HOUSE

Balenbouche is about 30 minutes' drive from Soufrière, in between Choiseul and Laborie. The first European settlement at Balenbouche was established in the mid-18th century when the land was cultivated and the original estate house was built.

Below: English engineering
Bottom: the ruins of the Balenbouche water wheel

Today, the great house stands on the site of two previous estate houses. It dates from the mid-19th century and is furnished with antiques from that period. The estate is a family-run guesthouse, restaurant and a thriving working plantation. Visitors can enjoy a walk along Balenbouche's nature trail or take a tour of the pretty gardens.

The land also includes a collection of ruins such as the slave quarters and the old plantation's sugar mill and water wheel with mechanical works that were shipped from England. The mill and the water wheel were used to process the sugar harvested on the plantation during the island's short-lived sugar boom.

There have been several significant archaeological discoveries made on the estate, including pre-Columbian petroglyphs, ceramics and stone tools.

Two dark-sand, rough beaches can be found on the property at nearby **Balenbouche Bay**, just a five-minute walk through the estate, and **Anse Touloulu**, a ten-minute walk.

LABORIE

The journey continues southeast skirting round and above **Laborie**, a small fishing community with wooden colonial buildings in its centre and some modern fishing huts on the edge of the water. The village also has the best beach in the area, pretty but quiet, populated by a handful of local fishermen. Laborie has a small selection of accommodation for visitors who prefer to stay away from the crowds and several good local restaurants.

TO THE INDUSTRIAL ZONE

The West Coast Road climbs out of Laborie up through the countryside and rural villages and then descends again into ★★ **Vieux Fort**, one of the oldest settlements at St Lucia's most southerly tip 67km (42 miles) from Castries. This busy, modern industrial town is often the first sight of the island for visitors because **Hewanorra International Airport** is located here, on the plains that open out to the sea. There are a few hotels, mainly B&Bs, not far from the airport, and some developed industry around the large port area, such as oil storage, warehouses and grain stores, and a wharf lined with shipping containers. Here, too, is one of the Eastern Caribbean's commercial-free-zone centres and a large fisheries complex, along with a busy, if slightly haphazard, shopping area.

EXPLORING VIEUX FORT

It isn't difficult to get around Vieux Fort, especially near the airport, where the roads are wider and well signed. Modern villas rub shoulders with fading French colonial-style buildings, reflecting the historical origins of the town's first French settlers. The older part of town is full of small grocery stores, typical Caribbean shops, takeaways and bakeries.

WINDSURFERS' PARADISE

Vieux Fort has a beautiful strip of white-sand beach, **Anse de Sables**, part of which can be seen

Star Attraction
● Vieux Fort

In the beginning
Hewanorra International Airport is named after an Amerindian word meaning "land of iguana". There have been significant archeological finds in the south of the island, where the airport is located.

French colonial architecture in Vieux Fort

Map
on pages
58–9

from the airport road. The waters just offshore are popular with windsurfers and kitesurfers who come to take advantage of the trade winds that bless this coast. There is a little bar and restaurant and a surf centre, where boards and equipment can be rented. A little further north is an all-inclusive resort.

Lighthouse with a View

★★ **Cap Moule à Chique** is a rocky outcrop with dry forest that towers high above the town and is as far south as you can get on the mainland. A little way out of the town centre, a tall lighthouse stands above Vieux Fort, overlooking the southern coast of the island for miles.

The drive up to the lighthouse requires a four-wheel drive vehicle and some nerve because of the twisting narrow path that leads up to a lookout, bordered by vegetation and sheer cliffs. Several residences dot the winding landscape and the peak. At the top next to the lighthouse is an electrical substation and a large antennae.

Standing 223m (730ft) above sea level, the 9m (29ft) **lighthouse** tower is believed to be the second highest in the world, because of its location perched on Cap Moule à Chique. Painted white with a red lantern at the top, the tower itself is closed to the public but the lighthouse site is not. From this vantage point the view is spectacular: to the northwest, beyond Vieux Fort, are the rolling hills and valleys of southern St Lucia, including the Pitons in the far distance, and **Morne Gomier**, a 313m (1,028ft)-high peak closer to town. To the northeast, just off the coast, you will see the rocky Maria Islands Nature Reserve *(see opposite)* poking out of the sea like seals. Here, too, are sweeping views up around the East Coast, where the waves of the Atlantic Ocean buffet the land and the rocks below.

On a clear day visitors to Cap Moule à Chique may also be able to spot the north coast of the island of St Vincent, which lies only 34km (21 miles) away from St Lucia.

Above: kitesurfing in the waters off Anse de Sables
Below: the deadly fer-de-lance snake

WILDLIFE ON THE ROCKS

★★ Maria Islands Nature Reserve (closed during the summer breeding season mid-May to end of July) lies 1.5km (1 mile) east of Vieux Fort, across a narrow ocean channel. From the mainland the islands look like small rocky outcrops. However, the two largest islets, Maria Major and Maria Minor, form the main part of the nature reserve, which covers 12 hectares (30 acres) of dry scrubland, characterised by a mixture of vegetation and cacti.

These compact islands on St Lucia's windward side have been shaped by the rough waves of the Atlantic, and are home to geckos and an array of rare bird and plant life. Noddies and terns have protected nesting sites here and lucky folks might spot the endemic St Lucia whiptail lizard *(Cnemidophorus vanzoi)* scuttling under bushes (the male has the colours of the national flag, *see page 17*), and the non-poisonous kouwess grass snake *(dromicus ornatus)*.

Access to the nature reserve is restricted to guided tours run by the St Lucia National Trust *(see page 42)* and to reach it from Vieux Fort visitors will need to take a small boat that ferries passengers across the channel. Tours set off from the National Trust's southern office in Vieux Fort (tel: 454 5014; email: natrust@candw.lc), where you can also find out more about the islands and their wildlife.

Star Attractions
● **Cap Moule à Chique**
● **Maria Islands Reserve**

Below: iguana country
Bottom: the Savannes Bay Nature Reserve

Map
on pages
58–9

A protected archaeological site once used by Amerindians, the islets are largely given over to the nature reserve but there is a small beach where visitors can enjoy a picnic and go swimming, snorkelling and diving offshore.

Below: Amerindian artefacts
Bottom: Savannes Bay
mangroves

SAVANNES BAY NATURE RESERVE

Back on the mainland, travelling north from Vieux Fort along the East Coast brings you to an area of mangrove swamp. The **★★ Savannes Bay Nature Reserve**, a protected wetland, encompasses the second-largest mangrove swamp in St Lucia, the first being the nearby **Mankoté Mangrove**, which lies a little further south on the coast. Mangrove swamps are expanses of brackish water where salt and fresh water meet. Trees and shrubs thrive in the nutrient-rich mud or salt flats.

The entire island's biodiversity makes St Lucia a valuable resource for environmentalists, and visitors can gain access, albeit restricted, to sites such as Savannes Bay, an ecosystem that remains virtually untouched by man. An extensive reef system runs from near the Maria Islands *(see page 81)* to the north end of the Savannes reserve, making snorkelling and diving along this section of the southeastern coast rewarding. The protective reef also allows for the cultivation of sea moss, which is grown on ropes under the water, suspended by hundreds of plastic bottles. Visitors also come here to see the bird life, such as herons, terns and egrets, that inhabit the rich mangrove swamp.

MILITARY PROTECTION

Until the 1960s the Mankoté Mangrove and forest were part of a US military base that stretched across more than 1,200 hectares (3,000 acres). Due to restricted access to the land, the mangrove swamp suffered little or no damage caused by development elsewhere. However, once the US vacated the land, the swamp was opened up to commercial fishermen and hunters, until it was granted reserve status by the government in 1986.

Nearby **Scorpion Island**, lying in the Savannes Bay, also contains red and black mangroves.

6: The East Coast

Vieux Fort – Mamiku Gardens – Praslin – Dennery – Castries

Map on pages 58–9

This route is approached via Vieux Fort, but it can just as easily be attempted from Castries in the north via the Transinsular Road.

THE WINDWARD SIDE

The East Coast Road from Vieux Fort is well made and follows a scenic route along the coastline of the windward side of the island. Some bridges were washed away in Hurricane Tomas, but these were under repair in 2011. This is the less commercial part of St Lucia with fewer large resorts and hotels than on the west coast, but with a wealth of nature reserves and walking trails through the rainforest, gardens and fishing hamlets.

Around 16km (9 miles) from Vieux Fort is **Micoud**, a small coastal village where, along with many other sites in the area, evidence of Amerindian settlement has been discovered.

The East Coast road crosses over the Troumassée River that skirts the edge of the fishing village, and clear signs direct drivers into Micoud proper. Inland is the starting and ending point for hikers attempting the walking trail that runs across the island through the Quilesse Forest and

> **Micoud Celebrations**
> The late Sir John Compton, St Lucia's first prime minister after Independence in 1979, was Micoud's MP for over 25 years. The village is an ideal place to visit during two of the island's biggest religious festivals, La Rose in August and La Marguerite in October. They are both celebrated with church services, street parades, delicious food and fun events.

Explore the rainforest

Map on pages 58–9

Birdwatching
There will be opportunities to spot tropical, sometimes rare, birdlife in St Lucia. When walking the trails and visiting the reserves, carry water, a hat, sunscreen and, if you have them, binoculars.

Edmund Forest reserves to Fond St Jacques, just outside Soufrière *(see page 74)*.

Alternatively, the circular Des Cartiers Rainforest Trail, at the start of the route, is about 4km (2½ miles) and takes 2 hours to complete. There are no steep hills, but the path can be muddy and slippery after rain. Guides at the Rangers' station can escort you. Parrot watching is good here in the early morning, but you must make arrangements with the Forestry Department (tours Mon–Fri 8.30am–3pm; entrance fee; tel: 468 5649; http://malff.com; *see page 104*) beforehand.

MAMIKU GARDENS

West of Micoud and north of the Troumassée River is **Latille Waterfall** (entrance fee), which has 6m (20ft) cascades that descend into a pool below; bring your swimsuit.

Driving north from Micoud the road heads inland, passing Malgrétoute, Patience and Mon Repos. ★★★ **Mamiku Gardens** (daily 9am–5pm; entrance fee; tel: 455 3729; email: shingletonsmithe@candw.lc) has 5 hectares (12 acres) of grounds surrounding an old estate house. It is located off the main road just north of Mon Repos in the Micoud Quarter, not far from Praslin Bay. In the 18th century Mamiku Estate was home to a French governor of the island; it later became a British military outpost during the tussle for ownership. By the early 20th century, it had fallen into neglect and the owners transformed it into its current role as a banana plantation.

TROPICAL TREATS

Visitors to the tropical gardens can explore the estate along a series of self-guided walking trails lined with orchids, heliconia and hibiscus and shaded by trees, including the gommier, which is still used to make dug-out canoes. One of the trails leads into the forest nearby. A small herb garden includes plants used in bush medicine introduced to the island by enslaved West Africans. Also on the site are ruins and archae-

Walking the rainforest trails can be tricky

ological artefacts. There is parking, a snack bar and a gift shop, and the ticket booth has trail maps.

PRASLIN BAY AND ISLAND

★ **Praslin Bay** is a beautiful deep bay divided into two sections by a small promontory which stretches out like a finger towards the tiny ★★ **Praslin Island** offshore. The St Lucian whiptail lizard was introduced here from the Maria Islands in 1995 to conserve the species (*see page 17*).

In the southern part of the bay, the village of Praslin maintains the fishing tradition on which it grew, and boat builders construct canoes from gommier trees using ancient techniques believed to have been imported by the first Amerindian settlers. In the northern half, construction on a luxury resort and golf course, Westin Le Paradis, has stalled.

The development is controversial because of the area's extensive red mangroves and mature trees, which are the habitat of the harmless endemic boa constrictor, a snake that can grow to over 3.5m (12ft). More than 30 species of bird live here and on the islands, such as the St Lucian oriole, the great white heron and the red-billed tropic bird.

Beyond the mangroves and dry forest is a cave network with evidence of an Amerindian settlement. Petroglyphs and remnants of ceramics and tools have been discovered along these parts.

Star Attractions
● Mamiku Gardens
● Praslin Bay

Bright orchids, beehive ginger and passionflowers decorate the island

Map
on pages
58–9 &
34–5

FREGATE ISLANDS NATURE RESERVE

Just off the coast at the northern perimeter of Praslin Bay is the ★**Fregate Islands Nature Reserve**. The two small islands that form the reserve, **Fregate Island Major** and **Fregate Island Minor**, have a combined size of less than ½ hectare (1 acre). The islands are named after the frigate bird (*fregata magnificens*), which nests and roosts here, migrating from Cape Verde in Africa, but unfortunately their numbers have dropped dramatically. The islands are covered mostly in xerophytic vegetation, cacti, mangrove forest and grass. The National Trust manages this reserve and Praslin Island, but tours have been suspended due to construction work in the area.

DENNERY BAY LOOKOUT

From Praslin Bay the East Coast Road continues north, following the coastline with wonderful views of the cliffs and hillside villages. It soon reaches **Dennery**, notable for its fishing industry.

The road bypasses the town, climbing up the hillside above it. Stop at the bar/restaurant on the roadside for an extensive view over **Dennery Bay**. Inland, along the Dennery River, is the **Rainforest Canopy Adventure** (daily 10am–4pm; reservations essential; tel: 458 0908; www.adventuretoursstlucia.com). Instructors strap you into

Bottom: frigate birds gather together

a harness and you descend the hillside on zip lines through the forest. Also on offer are bike tours along forest trails to the waterfall for bathing, offshore kayaking and a jeep safari, all with knowledgeable guides.

FOND D'OR BAY

About 1.6km (1 mile) from Dennery, where the main road turns west into the Mabouya Valley, is **Fond D'Or Bay**. This crescent-shaped bay has a beach of white sand, backed by sheer cliffs and a rugged landscape. Swimming is not recommended because of the rough sea, but the beach is lovely.

Driving from Dennery, the view of the bay from the roadside lookout point is spectacular. Nearby, an old fort and plantation ruins have been developed as **Fond D'Or Nature Reserve and Historical Park** (daily; entrance fee; tel: 453 3242), with a wooded canopy of coconut palms, an estuarine forest and mangrove wetlands. Visitors can hike along the forest trails and tour the estate that contains the remnants of the sugar mill, windmill and the old planter's house, which is now an interpretation centre. From one of the trails on the edge of the estate, walkers might spot the hill known locally as **Mabouya** or **La Sorcière** (the sorceress), which stands almost 7km (4 miles) away in the Castries Waterworks Forest Reserve.

TRANSINSULAR ROAD

The road now leaves the coast behind and heads inland and uphill into the forest before climbing over the **Barre de l'Isle**, the ridge which divides the island. At the high point is a stall where Forestry Department guides meet hikers. You can do the short Barre de l'Isle trail on your own, or hire a guide for the longer **Mount La Combe** hike. There were still roadworks in this area in 2011 repairing hurricane damage, so care is needed when driving. As you emerge from the forest the landscape becomes progressively more built up until the smell from the coffee-roasting factory notifies you that you have arrived on the outskirts of Castries again.

Star Attraction
● **Fregate Islands Nature Reserve**

Preserve and Protect
The St Lucia National Trust has managed the Fregate Islands and nearby forest area since 1989, when the land was awarded reserve status.

Dennery church overlooks the sea

Creole culture

St Lucia has a fascinating and complex culture steeped in the history and tradition of other lands. Like its highly seasoned Creole cuisine, the island and its people have created a virtual pepperpot culture, initially influenced by French and British colonists and enslaved Africans, that has become distinctively St Lucian. It is revealed in the melodic Kwéyòl language, the colourful art and literature, the festivals and music. The work of playwright and theatre director Roderick Walcott, writers such as Derek Walcott, Michael Aubertin and Gandolph St Clair, Robert Lee, Kendall Hippolyte, Charles Cadet, Stanley French, George Alphonse, Melania Daniel and MacDonald Dixon, plus artists Dunstan St Omer, Llewellyn Xavier, Virginia Henry and Corine George, and the folklorist and historian Harold Simmons are but a few examples of the depth of the island's artistic output.

LITERATURE

It is a wonder that such a tiny island has produced so many artists of note, who reveal much about the beauty of the language, landscapes and people through St Lucia's rich literary tradition. Caribbean people have always had an oral tradition; for centuries stories, tall tales and proverbs were passed on by word of mouth.

Before the 20th century Caribbean people were more often written about than doing the writing themselves, but that is no longer so. This island is the birthplace of Nobel Laureate Derek Walcott, born in 1930. His father was a civil servant who was also a talented watercolourist and his mother a respected headteacher. A poet, playwright, novelist and painter, Walcott came to prominence in the 1970s, although he began writing in his youth, as can be seen by his *Collected Poems 1948–1984*. In 1990 his St Lucian reworking of the Homeric legend in the poetic epic, *Omeros*, firmly established him as one of the world's greatest poets. In 1992 Walcott was

Bursting bamboo
A familiar sound at Christmas time in the rural hill areas is the loud crack of bamboo bursting. Traditionally young men hollow out a piece of bamboo, insert a stick and plug the bamboo with a kerosene-soaked rag. When lit the noise of the bamboo bursting can be heard far away. Another Christmas tradition is the equivalent of carol singers, who sing Creole songs to music from a *chak chak* band.

Opposite: Llewellyn Xavier's art
Above: souvenir dolls
Below: Derek Walcott

awarded the Nobel Prize for Literature. One of Walcott's best-known plays, *Dream on Monkey Mountain* (1970), has entertained audiences throughout the Caribbean, North America and the UK, and his most recent work, *White Egrets*, published in 2010, won the T.S. Eliot prize in 2011. Some of Walcott's stories and poems use motifs and imagery from the little fishing hamlets that he was familiar with as a boy, such as Soufrière and Gros Islet.

FOLKLORE

Below: carnival costumes are works of art and can be seen on display at St Lucia Distillers rum factory in Roseau valley

St Lucian folktales hailing from as far back as slavery times have survived to the present day, such as the *Tim Tim* tales, which are still told by a *kontè* or narrator. The stories of St Lucia have common elements found in tales from Africa and the rest of the Caribbean region, often only the names of the central characters have been changed. The island has a wealth of stories, riddles and proverbs about characters such as Konpè Lapin (rabbit), Konpè Makak (monkey), Konpè Chyen (dog) and Konpè Tig (tiger).

Today St Lucians recognise the value of their heritage through folktales and traditions, which are being preserved and revived. Characters such as the Toes, Papa Jab and his followers can be seen in masquerades at Christmas and New Year. The work of the Folk Research Centre (*see page 28*) has made an impact; it maintains an important historical archive, runs workshops for school children, organises festivals and events and promotes the use of Kwéyòl. Also influential is the work of Marie 'Sessenne' Descartes (1913–2010), a chantwelle (folk singer) whose Kwéyòl songs preserve St Lucian folk culture.

ART

Not only is the uniqueness of St Lucia expressed through its literature but also in its art such as that produced by Dunstan St Omer. His work can be seen displayed in public spaces all over the island, including religious artwork in the capital's city cathedral and over the altar at the tiny church in Jacmel. Several of St Omer's sons are also well known artists, who have collaborated with their father at some time.

Llewellyn Xavier is an internationally recognised artist and an active environmentalist, his abstract works, using oil on canvas, are a dazzling array of colour and texture often using Caribbean motifs reminiscent of the St Lucian landscape. He also produces original art using recycled materials. Xavier's work can be seen in collections in North America, the Caribbean and Europe *(see page 44)*.

St Lucia has no national gallery, but exhibitions of the work of local artists are mounted regularly. A selection of commercial galleries include:

Art and Antiques, Pointe Seraphine, Castries, tel: 459 0891. Commercial gallery exhibits the work of Llewellyn Xavier and other local and international artists.

Artsibit Gallery, corner of Brazil and Mongiraud streets, Castries, tel: 452 7865.

Caribbean Art Gallery, Rodney Bay Yacht Marina, tel: 452 8071. Commercial gallery displaying work by regional artists, maps and prints.

The Inner Gallery, Reduit Beach Avenue, Rodney Bay Village, tel: 452 8728. A selection of work by artists from St Lucia and the Caribbean.

Llewellyn Xavier Studio, Mount Du Cap, Cap

Cricket
The official cricket season runs from January to July when there are inter-island, regional and international matches. There is an impressive national cricket ground in Beausejour, Gros Islet, the venue for some of the Cricket World Cup matches in 2007. St Lucian female cricketers are valuable members of the women's West Indies team, but the men lagged behind until Darren Sammy was chosen for the West Indies tour of England in 2007. The Micoud-born cricketer was the first ever St Lucian selected for the men's senior team. Still the only St Lucian in the team, Sammy became captain of the West Indies in 2010 and led his team to the Cricket World Cup in 2011.

Below: detail of a wall mural depicting two drummers, Anse La Raye

Estate, tel: 450 9155. Showcase for the work of Llewellyn Xavier. View by appointment only.

CRAFTS

The African influence is best seen through the crafts and art produced on the island, particularly the woodcarvings of the island's craftsmen. Art in wood, of varying quality and size, can be found in artists' studios, markets and souvenir shops.

Choiseul is well-known for its distinctive clay pottery but here, too, artisans fashion fine hand-woven baskets that are sturdy enough to take to market and aesthetically pleasing enough for an excursion to the beach. The craft centre at Choiseul in southwest St Lucia sells the work of potters, basket-weavers and woodcarvers, who continue crafts handed down from generation to generation.

Sculptor and woodcarver Vincent Joseph Eudovic works at his Goodlands studio in the hills of Morne Fortune *(see page 33)*. His beautiful abstract carvings are created from local woods such as laurier mabouey, teak, mahogany and red and white cedar. His son, Jallim Eudovic, is also carving himself an international reputation. The ancient Indonesian art of batik is being preserved and given a Caribbean flavour at Caribelle Batik. Fabric is printed with bright images taken straight from St Lucian wildlife and natural landscapes.

The St Lucia Jazz Festival draws the crowds in May

FESTIVALS

St Lucians love to 'jump-up' (dance in the street), especially at a festival. The St Lucia Jazz Festival draws an international crowd, but it is at Carnival time in July, on Jounen Kwéyòl Entenasyonnal (International Creole Day) in October and during prominent festivals such as La Rose and La Marguerite that St Lucia's culture is revealed more fully.

Carnival time

CALENDAR OF EVENTS

1 January	New Year's Day
January	Nobel Laureate Week (3rd week)
22 February	Independence day
March/April	Easter Sunday (variable)
1 May	Labour Day
	St Lucia Jazz Festival (variable)
29 June	Fishermen's Feast (Fete Peche)
July	Carnival (variable)
1 August	Emancipation Day
30 August	Feast of St Rose De Lima (La Rose)
October	Thanksgiving Day (first Monday)
17 October	Feast of La Marguerite
25 October	Jounen Kwéyòl Entenasyonnal
December	Atlantic Rally for Cruisers
12 December	Festival of Lights
13 December	National Day
25 December	Christmas Day

MUSIC

The rhythms and beats of St Lucian music reflects the energy and creativity of the people and you will be entertained by folk music, cadence, zouk, calypso, steel pan, soca and reggae, country and western and US soul and R&B everywhere.

Folk songs by Marie 'Sessenne' Descartes, and Charles Cadet, the work of Ronald 'Boo' Hinkson and local calypsonians keep the oral tradition alive. In the bars and hotels you are more likely to hear reggae and soca. Cadence and zouk, with their origins in French and African rhythms, and calypso songs in Kwéyòl, are still performed by artists and remain popular here and on other French Creole-speaking islands.

FOOD AND DRINK

In almost every aspect of St Lucian culture there is a colourful blend of African, Amerindian, French and British influences, and nowhere more so than in its cuisine. The tropical climate and fertile soil mean that the island enjoys a near endless bounty of nature from cassava, sweet potato and dasheen to fragrant nutmeg, cinnamon and ginger. The landscape is punctuated with rich farmland where bananas, pineapple, grapefruit, oranges and mangoes grow in abundance. There is also superb seafood from the surrounding Caribbean Sea and Atlantic Ocean.

Seafood has a distinct and intense flavour here, most likely because it is served so fresh. Fish such as snapper, mahi-mahi (also known as dorado or dolphin), wahoo, flying fish and tuna are all available, as are crab, spiny lobster (in season 1 September to 30 April) and conch. The result is that mealtimes can often be a delicious cornucopia of fragrances and flavours.

LOCAL SPECIALITIES

Many of the foods the Amerindian settlers grew and consumed are still around today, notably cassava, sweet potatoes, yam, corn, peppers, okra, peanuts, cashew nuts and pumpkin. The Amerindians delighted in roasted corn, and today it remains a popular and healthy snack. The island's street vendors roast the corn on barbecues, often until it is black.

Cassava bread is a St Lucian staple, first enjoyed by the Amerindians and later the enslaved West Africans, who brought with them their own version of the bread. Served as an accompaniment to a main meal or as a filling snack, modern cassava bread comes in a variety of flavours from sweet or cherry to smoked herring.

The island's national dish is green fig and saltfish, a tasty meal of seasoned salt cod and small green bananas, known locally as a fig. Also worth a try is hearty pumpkin soup or callaloo soup made from the green leaf of the dasheen, a common root vegetable. The leaves have a spinach-like appearance and can also be cooked up with onions and saltfish.

Saltfish was first introduced to the Caribbean as an easy-to-store, inexpensive source of protein for the slaves working the land and it was they who created imaginative ways to cook it. Making the best of what was on offer and what they could afford has inspired generations of Caribbean cooks, so it is little wonder that menus include dishes made from almost every imaginable part of a pig or cow.

Pigs' tails are a local speciality, cooked in a juicy stew. Other stews include pepperpot – a combination of meats, vegetables and hot peppers with cassava juice – while souse bouillon contains salt beef cooked with a spicy mix of onions, beans, little dumplings and potatoes. Then there is cowheel soup and oxtail, chicken and beef, stewed, fried, baked or in mouth-watering curries.

Side dishes include breadfruit roasted, cut in slices or cubed in a salad, accras (spicy fishcakes), cassava, dasheen, sweet potato, yam, green fig, plantain, lentils, plain rice and rice and peas. These can be green or dried pigeon peas, black eye, split peas or lentils. Reflecting an Indian influence is roti, a flat unleavened bread wrap that contains a spicy meat, fish or vegetarian filling.

The island's food is flavoursome because of the seasonings used, of which onions, garlic, lime, peppers, thyme, ginger, clove, cinnamon and nutmeg are the most common. You will find a bottle of hot pepper sauce – made from scotch bonnet pepper – on almost every table, but be careful when adding it to your food as the strength of the sauce can vary greatly from mild to fiery.

FRUITS

Well-known for its small sweet bananas, the island also produces tropical fruits including guava, soursop, mango *(see page 97)*, papaya (paw paw), pineapple, orange, grapefruit, lime, passionfruit, tamarind and coconut. Fruit is everywhere, made in to juice, ice cream, a pickle or chutney.

SWEETS AND PASTRIES

The region's love affair with sugar stems back to the 17th-century plantation era when St Lucia began its sugar industry. Those with a sweet tooth won't be disappointed with a choice of sweets and pastries as different as tangy tamarind balls and coconut sugar cakes, cinnamon turnovers and banana bread. And don't forget the island fruit preserves such as guava jelly.

Rum: good for cocktails or straight up

WHAT TO DRINK

Refreshing fruit juices abound including orange, mango, pineapple, grapefruit, lime, guava and passionfruit.

Islanders are rightly proud of their rum. St Lucia Distillers produces a selection of dark and white rums at its factory in the Roseau Valley *(see page 55)*. The dark rums include Bounty, most commonly used in cocktails and punches, TOZ Gold and Elements 8 Gold. Connoisseurs can try the extra-aged Admiral Rodney and Chairman's Reserve. Crystal is a white rum, used in cocktails, while Denros is a double strength 160° proof rum (good for rubbing on aching joints even if you can't drink it).

In the island rum shops (known as *cabawe*) rum is drunk straight up or on the rocks, but the uninitiated can enjoy theirs in a blend of tropical fruit juices. There are also ready-made rum punches such as Smugglers rum punch, spiced rum such as Kwèyòl Spiced Rum and rum-based liquers such as Crème la Caye, Nutz & Rum (a peanut blend) and Orange Bliss. There are some 20 blended, flavoured or unadulterated rum products in all. Less potent is local Piton lager or shandy, which has an interesting flavour of sorrel or ginger.

Restaurants

You will never be far from somewhere to eat, but the greatest concentration of restaurants is in Rodney Bay, where a week's holiday is not long enough to try them all. Below is a selection of restaurants, divided into three categories according to the price of a main course:
$$$ = over US$30, $$ = US$15–30, $ = less than US$15.

Castries

Auberge Seraphine, Vigie Marina, tel: 453 2073; www.aubergeseraphine.com. A lovely place with an international menu, popular with business visitors and tourists. Overlooks the marina, best at twilight when you can watch the yachts, roosting egrets, and departing cruise ships. Open daily for breakfast, lunch and dinner. $$–$$$

The Coal Pot, Vigie Marina, tel: 452 5566; www.coalpotrestaurant.com. French cuisine with a Caribbean twist. One of the oldest restaurants, popular with local business people for lunch and visitors for dinner. Open Mon–Fri for lunch and dinner, Sat dinner only. $$

The Green Parrot Restaurant, Morne Fortune, tel: 452 3399. Established place with a European and Caribbean menu, a great view over Castries, and generous portions. Don't miss the green parrots. Open daily 7am–midnight. $$–$$$

Oceana Restaurant, Ridgeway House, La Toc Road, tel: 456 0300. Good food with an island twist and excellent service; views over Castries. Open daily for brunch, lunch, afternoon tea and dinner. $$–$$$

Rodney Bay and North

Big Chef, Rodney Bay, tel: 450 0210; www.bigchefsteakhouse.com. Popular, busy and with a great atmosphere, here you can eat the most tender, aged, Angus beef steaks plus a variety of seafood

> ### Mangoes
> Although there are more than 100 varieties of mango, just seven can be found in great numbers on St Lucia. Around 2,000 tons of the fruit are exported each year to as far afield as the UK. Of the seven common varieties only a few actually originate from St Lucia; they include the large juicy Cabishe, the Long and the Pa Louis mangoes. The sweet, orange-coloured Julie mango actually comes from Trinidad. Though closely associated with the region the mango, like the banana, is not indigenous. The fruit, be it sweet or tart, smooth or stringy in texture, can be juiced to produce a drink or made into ice cream or chutney.

and fish, accompanied by a good selection of international wines. The friendly waitresses design their own dresses, changing styles daily. An attached tapas bar opened in 2011, with a selection of appetizers, sherries and cigars. Open daily from 6pm. $$$

Buzz Seafood and Grill, Rodney Bay, tel: 458 0450; http://gosfest-st.lucia.tripod.com. Excellent seafood and steaks and imaginative local dishes such as lobster ravioli. Extensive wine list. Open Tue–Sun for dinner from 5pm and Sun brunch in season from 11am. $$–$$$

Jambe de Bois, Pigeon Island National Landmark, tel: 452 0321. Seafront cafe serving St Lucian specialities in the park. A pleasant place to take a break after hiking up the hill, to sit and watch the boating activity in the bay. $

Ku De Ta, Rodney Bay, tel: 458 4968; www.kudetastlucia.com. Down a leafy passage hung with lanterns and filled with Oriental art, the bar has a terrace for cocktails, and air-conditioned and alfresco areas for eating. Serves Asian food including a tasting menu served in a Bento Box. Open Mon–Sat for lunch, daily from 6pm for dinner. $$

Small but sweet

Bananas grown in St Lucia and its neighbours in the Windward Islands are smaller and (some say) sweeter than the larger fruit from elsewhere. The island is closely associated with the banana, a dominant crop for decades until the late 1990s (see page 15), when farmers were forced to begin diversifying crops. The plant takes 9–10 months to develop, and can propagate itself by producing suckers on its stem, which can be planted to produce another plant.

The Lime, near Reduit Beach, tel: 452 0761. Casual restaurant and bar with generous portions of local specialities such as breadfruit salad, spicy lentils, roti, and a meat and vegetarian dish of the day. Eat in or take away. Open daily 11am–2pm, 6.30pm–1am. **$–$$**

Spinnakers Beach Bar and Grill, St Lucia Yacht Club, Reduit Beach, tel: 452 8491. Unpretentious and authentic beach bar, perfect for lunch out of the sun, happy hour drinks or a relaxed seafront dinner. Creole fish, chicken, lobster, shrimp, stew beef, burgers and fries, salads and daily specials. Open for breakfast, lunch and dinner. **$**

Ti Bananne, Coco Palm Hotel, Rodney Bay, tel: 456 2866; www.coco-resorts. com. Independently run, but overlooking the hotel pool, the bar has sports TV and the restaurant offers one of the best breakfasts on the island, lunch and dinner, with a creole and international menu. Live music, open daily. **$$**

Marigot Bay

Chateau Mygo House of Seafood, Marigot Bay, tel: 458 3947; www.chateau mygo.com. Creole specialities with an East Indian twist; local vegetables, flying fish, mahi mahi, sushi and thin crust pizzas. Happy hour all day and night. Open daily for breakfast, lunch and dinner. **$$–$$$**

Doolittle's, Marigot Beach Club, tel: 451 4974; www.marigotdiveresort.com. Casual, elegant oceanside dining with a Creole-European menu including pumpkin soup, chicken roti, beef pepperpot stew and fish. Live entertainment three nights a week. Happy hour 5–7pm. **$$$**

Soufrière and Environs

Boucan, Hotel Chocolat, Rabot Estate, tel: 457 1624, www.thehotelchocolat. com. Themed restaurant on working cocoa plantation where the menu is cocoa-inspired for both sweet and savoury dishes, using locally-sourced, seasonal ingredients. Perched high up with spectacular views of the Pitons, the minimalist design allows you to concentrate on the gourmet food or your sunset cocktail. Open Wed–Sun noon–2.30pm, 6.30–9.30pm. **$$–$$$**

Dasheene, Ladera Resort, tel: 459 6600; www.ladera.com. Award-winning, elegant restaurant with innovative dishes using fresh local ingredients. Breathtaking views of the Pitons. Expensive but worth it. Open for breakfast, lunch, tea, dinner, Sun brunch. **$$$**

La Haut Plantation, West Coast Road, Soufrière, tel: 459 7008; www.la haut.com. Creole-influenced cuisine including fresh conch and spicy shrimp. On a hillside with a view of the Pitons and tables on the veranda. **$$–$$$**

The Mango Tree, Stonefield Estate, Soufrière, tel: 459 7037; www.stonefield villas.com. On the hillside with views of Petit Piton. Relaxed atmosphere with local dishes such as spicy roti, using homegrown organic produce. Vegan options. Barbecue and chak chak band on Thur. Open daily 7.30am–10pm. **$$–$$$**

Petite Peak, Bay Street, Soufrière, tel: 459 7838. Overlooking the waterfront, this was formerly the Old Courthouse, now a restaurant and bar on two floors, with fine dining downstairs and a bar and fast food upstairs. Local cuisine prepared by a local chef. Open daily 9am–11pm. $–$$$

Vieux Fort and South Coast

The Reef Beach Cafe, Anse De Sables, tel: 454 3418; www.slucia.com/reef. Casual beach cafe with Caribbean fare such as saltfish, bakes, seafood salad and T-bone steak; à la carte menu also available for dinner. Internet access and wheelchair access. $

East Coast

Whispering Palm, Fox Grove Inn, Mon Repos, tel: 455 3271; www.foxgrove inn.com. A good lunch stop. Eat indoors or on the balcony for lovely views down to the east coast. Varied menu with mussels, tuna, steak and lots of salads, including smoked duck. Open daily for breakfast, lunch and dinner. $$–$$$

Nightlife

Most hotels offer live music some nights a week, ranging from chak chak and jazz bands to piano bars, as well as nightclubs. There is a new casino in Baywalk Mall in Rodney Bay and a ten-screen cinema in the Choc area.

On the main street in Rodney Bay leading to Reduit Beach are bars such as the modern **Delirius** (tel: 451 3354; www.deliriusstlucia.com) with a bistro and dance floor. The bar manager, Alva Preville, won the 2010 Caribbean Tourism Association's competition for Bartender of the Year for his cocktails. At the junction further down the road are **The Triangle Pub** (karaoke on some nights) and **The Lime** (tel: 452 0761; music and dancing until late), the latter housing **Upper Level** (casual hangout with live entertainment and karaoke nights) upstairs. At the far end of the road is **Iguana Wanna** (tel: 450 9080), a bar, restaurant and nightclub on three floors.

The **Friday Night Jump-up** *(see page 40)* at Gros Islet hots up after 10pm. Street vendors and restaurants provide food – try barbecue chicken or fried fish washed down with an ice cold Piton lager. The event has a real party atmosphere and few people can resist the temptation to 'jump-up' and dance – the beats from the sound systems set up on the street are infectious.

Seafood Friday *(see page 57)* at Anse La Raye is an earlier evening fish fry. Tables are laid out for diners and loud reggae, calypso and kaiso music is pumped out of the bars. Most hotels organise an evening excursion to fish fries and local guides will escort you too. The village of Dennery has a **Fish Festival** on Saturday, while Canaries holds a **Creole Pot** on the last Saturday of the month, with a variety of local dishes, not just seafood.

In May the **St Lucia Jazz Festival** features an impressive line-up of international jazz and R&B artists and hosts day and evening events at venues including Derek Walcott Square in Castries, Fond d'Or Heritage Park and Pigeon Island National Landmark. For more information visit www.stluciajazz.org.

Friday Night Jump-up at Gros Islet

ACTIVE HOLIDAYS

WATER SPORTS
Diving

The coast of St Lucia is blessed with the warm water of the Caribbean Sea, with an average temperature of 24°C (75°F) and is the ideal place to scuba dive. Experienced divers can enjoy rich, colourful marine life just a few yards from the beach in some cases, while beginners can take to the water confidently with an expert instructor. The water here is home to angel fish and seahorses, octopus and turtles, black coral and spectacular sponges. Several shipwrecks around the coast provide fascinating artificial reefs in addition to the natural reefs.

Some of the island's most beautiful dive sites are located in protected marine areas such as the Soufrière Marine Management Area (SMMA), which extends from Anse Jambon to Anse L'Ivrogne near Gros Piton on the West Coast *(see page 65)*. The rise of tourism and its pollutant consequences and the need to maintain the fishing stock led the government to attempt to protect the fragile reefs in particular and the island's ecosystem in general.

The result is that St Lucia has become a popular Caribbean dive destination. In just a few days visitors can qualify as a certificated PADI or NAUI diver and experience the wonders of the deep.

On the West Coast near Soufrière are several excellent dive sites. **Anse Chastanet Reef** attracts novices and experienced divers. The marine life is just a short walk in the water from the volcanic sand beach, and there are caves to explore in the relatively shallow parts. Experienced divers can enjoy **Fairyland**, an interesting drift dive that can be affected by the area's strong currents. Here, too, is the Anse Chastanet resort and the base of Scuba St Lucia, which also has facilities for snorkellers.

Just outside Soufrière Bay is an exciting dive site known as **Key Hole Pinnacles** – four tall gorgonians that stand several hundred feet high but remain below the water.

Anse La Raye has a reef just off the beach and is believed by some to have

Water sports at Hummingbird Beach

the island's best wall and drift dives. Wreck divers are also catered for here. An artificial reef has been created by the deliberate sinking of an old freighter, the *Lesleen M*. The coral encrusted wreck, which stands in 18m (60ft) of water is overrun with colourful fish and is located near Anse Cochon and Anse La Raye.

Many of the larger hotels have dive centres on site, while others can offer dive and accommodation packages with independent operators. There are plenty of accredited dive centres on the island, which can provide thorough instruction and the opportunity to explore some of the best dive sites in the Caribbean.

Dive Fair Helen, Marigot Bay, tel: 451 7716, www.divefairhelen.com

Frog's Diving, Harmony Suites, Rodney Bay, tel: 458 0798, www.frogsdiving.com

Marigot Beach Club Hotel & Dive Resort, Marigot Bay, tel: 451 4974, www.marigotdiveresort.com

Scuba St Lucia, Anse Chastanet Resort, PO Box 7000, Soufrière, St Lucia, tel: 459 7755, www.scubastlucia.com

Snorkelling

You don't have to be an accomplished diver to enjoy St Lucia's reef system. A guided snorkel tour can provide a fascinating insight into tropical marine life. The guide will identify the many different kinds of fish and coral and will rent out equipment, unless you prefer to bring your own.

Snorkellers of all ages will find schools of colourful fish and other marine life around Anse Mamin, just north of Anse Chastanet and at Anse Cochon, south of Anse La Raye. North and south of Petit Piton, Malgretoute and Beausejour are also excellent spots for snorkelling.

If you are snorkelling independently be sure to stay close to the

> **West Coast Marine Areas**
> The west coast of St Lucia has four main protected Marine Reserve Areas (MRAS) that require a permit to dive. They are Anse Chastanet, Rachette Pointe, Petit Piton and Gros Piton, which also has very limited access. Divers can apply for annual or daily permits, which are available from the Soufrière Marine Management Area (SMMA) office (tel: 459 5500) in Soufrière, or any authorised dive operator.

beach and never underestimate the strength of the sea currents. Alternatively you can join a boat tour run by one of the island's dive operators. Tie a marker to one of your feet so that you are visible to passing boats.

River and Coastal Kayaking

Explore the island's rainforests and shady mangrove swamps by water. Guided kayaking tours are an exciting way to see the dense forest areas and wildlife. There are tours along the Roseau River and the western coastline, departing from Anse Cochon, south of Anse La Raye, and pitching up at Anse La Liberté *(see page 63)*. There are also kayaking trips around Pigeon Island National Landmark.

On the East Coast you can go kayaking in the Savannes Bay Nature Reserve to see the mangroves and hidden coves.

Dive Fair Helen, Marigot Bay, tel: 451 7716, www.divefairhelen.com

Island ATV Tours, Vieux Fort, tel: 712 7113/484 0896

Jungle Reef Adventures, Soufriere, tel: 459 7755, www.junglereefadventures.com

Windsurfing and Kitesurfing

The southern coast is a magnet for experienced and adventurous windsurfers and kitesurfers who are attracted by the challenge of the strong

Jungle Biking

Cycling along the forest and plantation trails at Anse Mamin Plantation can be a hair-raising experience and an exciting way to explore. Ride through groves of tropical fruit trees heavy with banana, mango and cocoa or visit the 18th-century ruins on the estate. The trails maintained by Bike St Lucia vary in difficulty from yellow (lower intermediate), red (intermediate) to black (expert). The most challenging ride is Tinker's trail, which has a steep uphill and fast downhill track.

winds that can whip up the Atlantic waves off Anse de Sables at Vieux Fort. Kitesurfing is a mixture of paragliding, wakeboarding, surfing and windsurfing, but can be learned on dry land.

The best winds blow from December to June, when the trade winds are most consistent and they blow strongly cross-onshore from the left. Luckily the Moule à Chique peninsula will prevent you from being blown off into the Atlantic. However, you may still catch a good breeze in the summer months.

Anse de Sables is a long stretch of pretty white sand with a beach bar/cafe, public toilets and shower facilities. Next to the cafe is Reef Kite and Surf, which has plenty of equipment for rent and offers windsurfing and kiteboarding instruction. The centre has good links with several hotels on the island.

Elsewhere, Cas-en-Bas in the northeast is also a popular spot and there are facilities here too. Windsurf sails zipping across the water are a sight to behold. Less experienced windsurfers may prefer the relatively quiet Caribbean Sea on the west coast.

You can rent windsurf boards or kitesurfing equipment, and take lessons at the water sports facilities

of the larger hotels and resorts, as well as through dive operators.

Kitesurfing St Lucia, Cas-en-Bas, Gros Islet, tel: 714 9589, www.kitesurfingstlucia.com

The Reef Kite and Surf, Anse de Sables Beach, Vieux Fort, tel: 454 3418, www.slucia.com/windsurf; www.slucia.com/kitesurf

Fishing

The warm Caribbean waters are teeming with fish and, depending on the time of year, you could reel in big game fish such as marlin, wahoo, kingfish, sailfish and dorado (mahi mahi, also known as dolphin); tuna and barracuda can also be caught in these waters.

Deep sea or sport fishing is very popular and every year there are numerous events and competitions attended by local and visiting fishermen. The 3-day St Lucia Bill Fishing Tournament is held in September. Most operators follow a catch and release code.

Visitors can book an entire day or a half-day fishing trip where they may also spot turtles, dolphins and whales in season. For more information visit www.worldwidefishing.com/stlucia/salt.htm

Captain Mike's, Vigie Marina, Castries, tel: 452 7044, http://captmikes.com

Hackshaws Boat Charters, Vigie Marina, tel: 453 0553, www.hackshaws.com

Trivial Pursuit Charters, Vigie, Castries, tel: 720 4001, www.casadelvega.com

Whale Watching

Whales are cetaceans, some of the largest mammals in the world. Around this tiny island, many species of resident and migratory whales can be seen in the warm Caribbean Sea. The various species can be seen at different times of year, especially during the migratory mating season from October to April. Most common are

sperm whales, pilot whales, hump-back whales and false killer whales. Common, spinner, spotted, striped and bottlenose dolphins can also be spotted accompanying the whales, sometimes leaping above the water.
Captain Mike's, tel: 452 7044, http://captmikes.com
Hackshaws Boat Charters, tel: 453 0553, www.hackshaws.com

Sailing

An exciting way to explore the coast and see the scenic landscape is by boat. Boat tours can include a spot of diving, snorkelling, swimming or sport fishing, and can be day or sunset party cruises. Full- and half-day sails can be arranged through one of the local boat charter companies based at the marina at Castries, Rodney Bay Marina, Marigot Bay and Soufrière.

Depending on the time of year St Lucia hosts numerous sailing events, many of them beginning or ending at Rodney Bay Marina. The St Lucia Regatta is a five race series while the Atlantic Rally for Cruisers (*see pages 39 and 40*) is an annual race from the Canary Islands to St Lucia.
Endless Summer Cruises, tel: 450 8651, www.stluciaboattours.com

Liana Ransom, Rodney Bay Marina (*see page 64*), tel: 452 8644, www.seaspraycruises.com
Mystic Man Tours, Bay Street, Soufrière, tel: 459 7783, www.mysticmantours.com
St Lucia Yacht Club, tel: 452 8350, www.stluciayachtclub.com

CYCLING

Tours by bike can be challenging but rewarding for visitors who want to get close to nature, since a bike can get to places a motor vehicle cannot. There are mountain bike trips through the interior, exploring the trails that run through the scenic countryside and dense beautiful forest, and stopping for a dip in a cooling waterfall. Trips from Rodney Bay to the far north provide an opportunity to view the spectacular rugged Atlantic coast, while trips to the Soufrière area take in the banana plantations, Botanical Gardens and Sulphur Springs.

Not for the faint hearted are the bike trails that cut through the lush vegetation on the Anse Mamin Plantation. Bike St Lucia has trails for the beginner and the professional mountain biker.

Cycling around town

Bike St Lucia, tel: 457 1400, www.bike stlucia.com
Palm Services Rainforest Cycling Adventure, tel: 458 0908, www.adventure toursstlucia.com

HIKING

Exploring the island interior on foot is one way to experience some of the breathtaking scenery that makes up the volcanic island's landscape. With almost year round warm sunshine and summer temperatures rising above 31°C (88°F), the high mountain and forest areas, where it is several degrees cooler, provide walkers with welcome relief from the heat.

St Lucia has 77 sq km (30 sq miles) of protected forest land, which is the natural habitat of rare plants, trees, birds and wildlife. As a result walking tours are permitted only with an official guide. Forest walks and hikes vary in difficulty.

Rainforest Trails

The **Edmund Forest Reserve** in St Lucia's heartland can be approached from the west. The journey takes you through small country hamlets, along bumpy potholed roads and affords views of the magnificent Mount Gimie before finally reaching the forest area, the entrance of which has a manned ranger station and a public toilet. A 3-hour hike along the reserve's strenuous walking trails leads deep into the forest, where you can enjoy the shade of tall ferns, blue mahoe, bamboo and mahogany laced with bromeliads, lianas and orchids. You can also see fabulous flora and fruit such as the bird of paradise, brightly coloured heliconia and hibiscus, banana and pineapple plants.

Visitors need to be fit to attempt the 4km (2½-mile) **Enbas Saut Forest Trail**, which takes walkers down 2,112 steps to two cascades of mountain fresh water that flow into clear

Horse Riding

Touring the picturesque Atlantic coast on horseback can be fun and everyone likes to ride on the beach. However, be aware that these lean ponies are not kept to European and North American standards and are worked hard. Check for signs of lameness and sores caused by rough ground, rasping sand or salt water chafing against harness. Their excrement fouls the beach for other users and pollutes the water when the sea eventually cleans it up, raising nitrogen levels and causing algae to choke coral.

pools below, and beyond to the Troumassée River and the hamlet of Micoud on the East Coast.

Nearby the lush canopied **Quilesse Forest Reserve** is the habitat of the rarely seen St Lucia parrot *(Amazona versicolor),* known locally as jacquot. The walking trails through this reserve can also provide glimpses of other indigenous island wildlife.

The moderately taxing **Barre de L'Isle Trail** (1.6km/1 mile) cuts through the forest in an east to west direction and provides unforgettable panoramic views over the Cul-de-Sac and Mabouya valleys and out to the Atlantic Coast.

A short drive (30 minutes) southeast of Castries is the 5km (3-mile) **Forestierre Trail**. It follows an old French road through a mature forest with lush ferns and fig trees.

In the forest heartland is the 3km (1¾-mile) trail through the **Millet Bird Sanctuary**, with several species of rare bird. For more information about the island's forest reserves and other national heritage sites or to book a trail hike contact:
St Lucia Forestry Department, tel: 468 5649 (Union), 457 1427 (Soufrière), http://malff.com
St Lucia Heritage Tours, tel: 458 1454, www.heritagetoursstlucia.org

BIRDWATCHING

With such vast forested areas and a mountain landscape, visitors to St Lucia can spot some of the region's colourful and rare, indigenous and migratory birds. With patience and luck you may see some wonderful tropical birds such as the endangered St Lucia wren *(Troglodytes aedon mesoleucus)*, St Lucia black finch *(Melanospiza richardsoni)*, the white breasted thrasher *(Ramphocinclus brachyurus sanctaeluciae)* and the national bird, the St Lucia parrot *(Amazona versicolor)*, with its bright blue face, green wings and a red patch across the throat and chest.

Several forest areas throughout the island are especially good for birdwatching, including the Millet Bird Sanctuary, Edmund Forest Reserve, Quilesse Forest Reserve , Grand Anse, Grand Bois Forest, Maria Islands Nature Reserve, Savannes Bay Nature Reserve and the Monkoté Mangrove swamp.

Birdwatching tours are best arranged through the Forestry Department (tel: 468 5649).

JEEP SAFARI & ATV TOURS

Island excursions by sturdy open-top jeep through the forest and rural hill areas is an exciting way to see St Lucia. And racing through plantation land on an all-terrain vehicle (ATV) adds a touch of adventure to any trip.
ATV Paradise Tours Ltd, Fond Estate, Micoud, tel: 455 3245, www.atvstlucia.com
Island ATV Tours, Vieux Fort, tel: 712 7113/484 0896

GOLF

There is an 18-hole championship golf course at Cap Estate in the far north of the island. Clubs, balls and shoes can be hired, and 40-minute lessons are available on the driving range.
St Lucia Golf Club, Cap Estate, Rodney Bay, tel: 450 8523, www.stluciagolf.com

TENNIS AND SQUASH

Most large resorts have courts that can be rented by the hour, and offer lessons.
Rex St Lucian Hotel, Rodney Bay, tel: 452 8351, www.rexresorts.com. There are floodlit tennis courts available to guests and non-guests of the hotel.
St Lucia Racquet Club, Smugglers Cove, tel: 450 0106. Tennis courts and a squash court.

ATV Paradise Tours in action

PRACTICAL INFORMATION

Getting There

BY AIR

Long distance scheduled and charter flights, such as trans-Atlantic flights, fly in to **Hewanorra International Airport** (UVF) at Vieux Fort in the south, 67km (42 miles) from Castries. If you are staying at a hotel in the far north of the island be prepared for a scenic journey of up to 2 hours to get to your destination.

The frequency of flights varies according to the season and many charter flights stop in the summer months and in the hurricane season. Schedules usually change mid-April.

Another, smaller airport, the **George F.L. Charles Airport** (SLU) is located at Vigie, on the outskirts of Castries, which receives inter-island flights. Airlines using the Vigie airport include LIAT, Air Caraïbes, Winair and American Eagle.

There is a helicopter shuttle from Hewanorra to George F.L. Charles Airport. It is not a cheap option but it does cut travelling time right down

Adventure by jeep

to 10 minutes for the trip between the two airports.

St Lucia Helicopters Ltd, tel: 453 6950; www.stluciahelicopters.com

From the US

There are direct flights from JFK New York with Jet Blue and American Airlines, from Miami with American Airlines, from Charlotte with US Airways and from Atlanta with Delta.

From Europe

Virgin Atlantic flies three times a weeks and British Airways flies daily from London Gatwick. Thomas Cook Airlines (formerly Condor) flies weekly from London Heathrow via Frankfurt.

From Canada

Air Canada, Air Transat, Canjet, Sunwing and WestJet fly from Toronto. Air Canada flies from Montréal.

From the Caribbean

The airlines Air Caraïbes, LIAT, Winair and SVG Air fly from neighbouring islands, while American Eagle flies

from Puerto Rico for connections with US cities.

Air Caraïbes, tel: 451 6364; www.air caraibes.com

LIAT, tel: 452 3056; www.fly-liat.com

Winair, tel: 451 7269; www.fly-winair.com

SVG Air, www.svgair.com

American Eagle, tel: 454 6777, www.aa.com

BY SEA

Ferry

L'Express des Iles has a high-speed catamaran car ferry service linking St Lucia with Dominica and the French islands of Martinique, Guadeloupe, Les Saintes and Marie Galante, usually crossing three times a week. Travelling time is short enough to justify hopping over to a neighbouring island for a day or even a weekend. Avoid island hopping on the day you are leaving St Lucia because there is no guarantee that your ferry will return in time for you to make an airline connection. The agent in St Lucia, **Cox & Company Ltd**, has an office at the ferry terminal on La Toc Road in Castries (Mon–Fri 8am–4.15pm, tel: 456 5022/23/24, www.express-des-iles.com).

Cruises

St Lucia is a popular port of call for cruise ships starting from Florida, San Juan, Puerto Rico and Barbados. The port of entry is Castries and the view across the bay as the ship approaches is stunning. Cruise ships dock at Pointe Seraphine or Place Carenage, either side of Castries harbour, and there is duty-free shopping at both locations.

TOUR OPERATORS

There are dozens of British and North American tour operators offering holiday packages in St Lucia. Go to your local travel agent or find them on the internet.

Getting Around

BY ROAD

Buses

The public bus system in St Lucia operates from early in the morning until early evening. It is safe to say that more buses run in the morning and that the frequency tends to tail off after the end of the working day. Castries and Vieux Fort have the best services, but the more remote rural areas aren't always as well served. If you go to Soufrière by bus, it is usually quicker and easier to return via Vieux Fort, where there are better connections.

Buses can be distinguished from other minibuses by their licence plates, which begin with the letter M. The routes are zoned and priced accordingly, so a short hop costs EC$1.50, while a longer trip from Castries to Soufrière costs EC$8; you must have the exact fare. In Castries, buses for the north of the island leave from a terminus behind the market on Darling Road; buses for Anse la Raye and the west coast road leave from the south side of the market; buses for Dennery and Vieux Fort leave from Hospital Road by the river.

If you do travel on the bus you will hear local people call out "one stop" when they want to get off. Once you are familiar with the route, you could try it yourself. Alternatively, ask the driver to let you know when you reach your destination.

Taxis

Taxis are available in the form of a saloon vehicle or a minivan that can accommodate a small group. They are plentiful at the airports, in the resort areas at hotels, at shopping malls and in town at the official stands. Look for the TX licence plate. Taxis are not metered because fares are fixed and the majority of drivers tend to stick to the published rates.

However, check the fare before setting off and make sure you are being quoted in EC dollars. A taxi from Rodney Bay to Gros Islet costs EC$25 (US$10), from Castries to Soufrière EC$239 (US$90), Castries to Vieux Fort EC$199 (US$75).

A taxi is the obvious choice for a hotel transfer to and from the airport, unless your hotel offers a shuttle service. You can also arrange for a taxi driver/guide to take you on an island tour, on a shopping trip, or on an excursion to the Friday Night fish fry at Anse La Raye and the Jump-up at Gros Islet. Some reliable and knowledgeable local drivers and taxi services include:

Allan Sampson, tel: 452 2651.
Ben's Taxi Service, on the west coast, tel: 459 5457/7160
Francis Sanganoo, North Lime Taxi Association, Rodney Bay, tel: 487 4953; email: nltaxi@hotmail.com
Julian Bissette, tel: 284 5476
Macarinus Charlemagne, tel: 485 9213
Randall Austin, tel: 719 9432, email: randalltaxi@hotmail.com

Car Rental

In St Lucia you drive on the left. Visiting drivers must be over 25 years old and should possess an international driver's licence (with an official stamp from the Immigration Department) or obtain a temporary driving permit, which is valid for three months, by presenting a current driving licence at the main police station (Bridge Street, Castries). The car rental company can also process a temporary permit, for which there is a charge of US$21 (EC$54). The wearing of seat belts is compulsory.

There is a choice of car rental companies and several, such as West Coast Jeeps, will deliver the vehicle to your hotel and collect it at the end of the

rental period. The following listing is just a small selection.

Alexo Car/Avis, tel: 452 2700; www.avisstlucia.com
Cool Breeze Jeep-Car Rental, tel: 459 7729; www.coolbreezecarrental.com
Hertz, tel: 452 0679; www.hertz.com
West Coast Jeeps and Taxi Service, tel: 459 5457; www.westcoastjeeps.com

BY SEA
Ferries

There are several local ferries which shuttle passengers around the island. In Castries there is the shuttle service across the harbour from La Place Carenage to Pointe Seraphine. In Rodney Bay a ferry shuttles between the marina, the village and Pigeon Island.

In Marigot Bay the Gingerbread Express plies back and forth between Doolittle's Restaurant and the end of the road, while the solar-powered Sunshine Express links the Discovery Resort with the beach and restaurants around the bay. Water taxis are a common sight in Soufrière and are the easiest way of getting from the waterfront to Anse Chastanet beach because the road is in a state of disrepair. You can also book a shuttle from Rodney Bay or Castries to Soufrière, which takes only 40 minutes and is quicker than going by road.

Etiquette

As in the Caribbean in general, good manners go a long way in St Lucia. "Please", "thank you", and a respectful and friendly demeanour are expected from everyone. "Hello", "goodbye", "good morning" and "good night" are used in every situation be it your hotel, a local bar, a restaurant or when passing strangers on the road. If you need to ask directions or advice always greet the person before asking a question. Don't take anyone's picture without first asking permission and don't refer to island residents as "natives".

Facts for the Visitor

BUSINESS HOURS

Banks are generally open Monday to Thursday 8am–2pm, and until 5pm on Friday.

CURRENCY

The official currency of St Lucia is the Eastern Caribbean dollar (EC$), which is pegged to the US dollar. The US dollar and all major credit cards and travellers' cheques are accepted in most places including restaurants and shops, especially in the resort areas.

EC dollars are produced in denominations of $100, $50, $20, $10 and $5 notes and $1, 25¢, 10¢, 5¢, 2¢ and 1¢ coins.

There are foreign exchange and banking facilities in Castries, Rodney Bay, Vieux Fort, Soufrière and at Hewanorra International Airport, which is usually open from 12.30pm until the last flight leaves.

CUSTOMS

It is prohibited to enter St Lucia with illegal drugs or firearms. Duty-free allowances for travellers visiting the island are 200 cigarettes or 250 grams of tobacco and 1 litre of wine or spirits.

DEPARTURE TAX

Since January 2008, all taxes have been included in air ticket prices. If leaving by sea, on the ferry, there is a departure tax of EC$33.

DIPLOMATIC REPRESENTATION

British High Commission, 2nd floor Francis Compton Building, Waterfront, Castries, tel: 452 2484; email: britishhc@candw.lc
US Embassy, located in Barbados, at the Canadian Imperial Bank of Commerce (cibs) Building, Broad Street, Bridgetown, tel: (246) 436 4950/429 5246.

ELECTRICITY

220 volts, 50 cycles AC and 110 volts, 60 cycles AC.

EMERGENCIES

Police **911**
Fire and Ambulance **911**
The main police station is located on Bridge Street, Castries (tel: 452 2854). In Rodney Bay the police station is beside the St Lucia Yacht Club on Reduit Beach.

ENTRY REQUIREMENTS

Passports are required for entry to St Lucia, except for British, French, Canadian and US citizens on short visits (weekend to one week) holding return tickets. US citizens do however need a passport for re-entry into the US and passports are highly recommended for ease of access into St Lucia for everyone. For visa requirements, other information and updates, see www.stlucia.gov.lc.

FACILITIES FOR THE DISABLED

Facilities for disabled visitors are few, although some of the newer and larger hotels and resorts will be better equipped. In Castries and elsewhere the curbs and pavements can be high and difficult for wheelchair users and the physically challenged to negotiate, but there are many accessible visitor attractions. Check in advance that your hotel has the facilities you require and that the places you want to visit can accommodate you.

GUIDED TOURS

Barefoot Holidays, Rodney Bay, tel: 450 0507; www.barefootholidays.com
St Lucia Reps/Sunlink Tours, Reduit Beach Avenue, Rodney Bay, tel: 456 9100/1-800-SUNLINK; www.sunlinktours.com
Spice Travel, Reduit, tel: 452 0865/6; www.casalucia.com

Travel Boutique, Top floor, Adjodha Building, Laborie Street, Castries, tel: 451 6364; www.the-travel-boutique.com

MEDIA

Print

St Lucia has five newspapers including *The Star* and *The Voice* which are published three times a week. The *Crusader*, *The St Lucia Mirror*, *The Vanguard* and *One Caribbean* are all weeklies available across the island.

Tropical Traveller, a monthly magazine, promotes restaurants and gives information about upcoming events, and a biannual magazine, *Visions of St Lucia*, has listings and features about the island's attractions. Both are distributed through hotels.

TV

There are six local television channels, including Helen TV and DBS. St Lucia also receives a host of programmes from the US via satellite.

Radio

The island has four radio stations: Radio St Lucia, Radio 100, Radio Caribbean International and Hot FM, which broadcast local news and music.

MEDICAL SERVICES

The main public medical facility on the island is the large Victoria Hospital in Castries (tel: 452 2421), which has a 24-hour emergency department. Private hospitals include St Jude's Hospital in Vieux Fort (tel: 454 6041) and the small Tapion Hospital in the south of Castries (tel: 459 2000; www.tapion_hospital.com), both having emergency services available to visitors. Elsewhere there are medical centres and clinics in Soufrière (tel: 459 7258/ 5001) and Dennery (tel: 453 3310).

POSTAL SERVICE

The main post office in the capital, Castries, is located on Bridge Street; there you can buy stamps and phonecards. Rodney Bay Mall and Gablewoods Mall have post office counters. There are also small post offices in most towns and generally they are open Monday to Friday 8.30am–4.30pm.

PUBLIC HOLIDAYS

1 January: New Year's Day
2 January: New Year's Holiday

Shopping in Castries

22 February: Independence Day
March/April (variable): Easter
1 May: Labour Day; Whitsun (variable); Corpus Christi (variable)
1 August: Emancipation Day
1 October: Thanksgiving
13 December: National Day
25 December: Christmas Day
26 December: Boxing Day

SECURITY AND CRIME

St Lucia is a relatively safe island but crime, especially petty theft, certainly exists. By all means relax while on holiday but don't leave home without your common sense. Keep an eye on personal possessions and important documents when wandering in the markets and the busy resort areas; keep your money in a safe place, and leave your expensive jewellery at home or in the hotel safe. If you are renting a car keep valuables out of sight, preferably locked in the boot, and don't offer lifts to strangers. Avoid the beaches and out of the way side streets after dark.

It is likely that you will be approached by vendors offering anything from hair braiding to crafts and a variety of souvenirs on the beach and at tourist attractions. If you are interested in what's on offer then haggle for an agreeable price, but if not don't waste people's time. A firm but polite "no thank you" is usually sufficient to deter any further advances.

TELEPHONE & COMMUNICATIONS

Calls home from your hotel can be prohibitively expensive so it is advisable to make calls from public payphones, if you have change, or a calling station where you can use prepaid phonecards. The LIME (Landline, Internet, Mobile, Entertainment) office on Bridge Street in Castries, near the post office, has public telephones and sells a wide selection of phonecards. Both

Shopping in Castries

Saturday is market day in the capital and Central Market and the Vendors' Arcade keep a brisk pace. Pointe Seraphine is a modern mall at the cruise ship terminal, with public telephones, an ATM and a cafe. On sale are designer goods and locally made crafts and art at Bagshaws, Art and Antiques and Lava Flow. St Lucia Jazz Festival tickets are also available from a booth here. Across the harbour is La Place Carenage precinct, which is more convenient for the market. Remember your passport and airline ticket for duty-free shopping.

Digicel and LIME have offices in Baywalk Mall, Rodney Bay.

Mobile phones can be rented from specialist suppliers and are operated by Digicel and LIME. If you bring your own phone from home you can choose whether to select Digicel or LIME networks.

There are internet cafes and facilities throughout the island, in the resort areas and in shopping centres. Most hotels have computers for guests' use and internet access for those with laptops.

The international country code for St Lucia is **758**.

TIME ZONE

Four hours behind Greenwich Mean Time in the winter, five hours when Daylight Saving Time applies.

TIPPING

Be prepared to pay a 10 percent service charge and 8 percent government tax on all goods and services supplied by hotels and restaurants. In particular most restaurants and hotels will often automatically add a 10–15 percent service charge to your bill, so no further gratuity is necessary unless you would like to tip an especially attentive waiter or another member

Getting Married in St Lucia

An increasing number of couples choose to tie the knot while on holiday in St Lucia. That way they can combine the wedding and honeymoon, and even bring friends and relations along too.

Couples can opt to have their nuptials barefoot on the beach, in a small island church, or at a national landmark, such as Diamond Botanical Gardens, Pigeon Island National Landmark or at the foot of the Pitons.

Tour operators in the UK and USA offer all-inclusive wedding and honeymoon packages, while larger hotels have a dedicated wedding planner, who can arrange every detail, whether it's a simple ceremony or a lavish family affair.

Before the wedding couples will need to be resident on St Lucia for three days. However, after two days a local lawyer can begin the process and apply for a licence on the couple's behalf – it needs to be applied for at least two working days before the ceremony.

Documents required before the wedding can take place are:
• A valid passport
• Birth certificate
• Divorcees should bring their Decree Absolute
• Widows/widowers should bring the death certificate of their spouse and also their original marriage certificate
• A deed poll is required if there has been a name change
• If the bride or groom is under 18 the parents must provide their consent in a sworn affidavit stamped by a Notary Public

Tips for a troublefree tropical wedding:
• Choose your wedding outfit carefully, the heat can play havoc with your hair and clothing.
• Check that the airline can transport the wedding clothes safely, either boxed or in a protective garment bag. Also contact the hotel in advance regarding pressing delicate fabrics.
• Choose your photographer wisely, as photographs and a video of the event could be your only mementoes.

of staff. Where service is not included a tip of 10–20 percent is appropriate.

TOURIST INFORMATION

The St Lucia Tourist Board has branches in the UK and North America where you can pick up brochures and information about the island. The Tourist Board's administrative office is in Castries, but there are information booths at Hewanorra and George F.L. Charles airports, Pointe Seraphine and Place Carenage seaports in Castries and on Bay Street in Soufrière.

TOURIST BOARD OFFICE IN ST LUCIA

PO Box 221, Sureline Building, Vide Bouteille, Castries, tel: 452 4094; www.stlucianow.com

TOURIST BOARD OFFICES ABROAD

Canada, 65 Overlea Boulevard, Suite 250, Toronto, Ontario M4H 1P1, tel: (416) 362 4242; email: sltbcanada@aol.com
UK, 1 Collingham Gardens, London SW5 0HW, tel: 020 7341 7000; email: sltbinfo@stluciauk.org
USA, 800 Second Avenue, 9th Floor, New York, NY 10017, tel: (212) 867 2951/2950; email: stluciatourism@aol.com

WHAT TO WEAR

Stick to cool and comfortable attire in the heat. Wearing skimpy shorts, skirts or beachwear while sightseeing and shopping in town is considered inappropriate. Most restaurants prefer their guests to dress elegantly casual, however some of the more upmarket establishments may require men to wear a jacket and occasionally a tie.

In winter the evenings can be cool, as can the air-conditioning, so it's best to carry a light cardigan or wrap; don't forget to take a lightweight umbrella or raincoat to protect you from brief showers during the rainy season.

ACCOMMODATION

St Lucia has a reputation for expensive all-inclusive accommodation but in fact there is a choice of places to stay, with something for every budget from large, exclusive all-inclusive resorts to small, intimate inns and basic bed and breakfasts. Self-catering apartments and luxury villas are also available to rent.

Basic bed and breakfasts run by St Lucians who open up their homes to visitors are popular with budget-conscious travellers who don't mind staying off the beaten track and don't need the creature comforts offered by the upmarket resorts.

The beauty of staying with a local family is that you will have the chance to experience first hand the real St Lucia. Local people will also be able to point you in the direction of little-known sights and the best places to enjoy authentic Creole cuisine. If you are staying in a rural area or far from reliable public transport links you are best advised to rent a sturdy vehicle, or employ a guide because taxi fares can mount up.

The wild side of the island is never far away from the splashy hotels and resorts, in fact most have made a feature of the bays, valleys and forests where they are situated. There are even some rustic places with accommodation that will satisfy eco-tourists and lovers of the outdoors who want to get close to nature.

Off-season rates (mid-April to mid-December) can be substantially lower than high-season rates (mid-December to mid-April). Be prepared to pay a 10 percent service charge and a government tax of 8 percent, but for all-inclusive package holidays this may already be included in the price you are quoted. Rates are subject to change, so always check in advance.

The price categories quoted below are for a double room a night in high season. European and American meal plans are available. Most resort hotels will provide an all-inclusive price on request, otherwise your travel agent can supply you with a quote.

$$$$ Luxury = above US$500
$$$ Expensive = US$200–500
$$ Moderate = US$100–200
$ Inexpensive = under US$100

CASTRIES

Auberge Seraphine, Vigie Cove, Castries, tel: 453 2073; www.auberge seraphine.com. Small city hotel close to George F.L. Charles Airport and central Castries. Simple accommodation with view of the harbour. Swimming pool and beach shuttle available for guests. **$$**

Eudovic Guest House, Goodlands, Castries, tel: 452 2747; email: eudovic@ candw.lc. Small, friendly guesthouse run by local artist and woodcarver Vincent Eudovic and his family. Ten minutes from Castries' centre. Rooms are simple with lovely furniture made from local wood, a kitchenette and fan. The artist's studio is at the same property. **$**

Green Parrot Hotel, Morne Fortune, tel: 452 3399/452 3167. Large, comfortable rooms in a well-established hotel, with good views over Castries. The hotel has a popular and well-known restaurant. **$**

Rendezvous Resort, Malabar Beach, tel: 452 4211; www.theromanticholiday.com. Couples-only all-inclusive, medium-sized hotel popular for weddings and honeymoons. Set in pretty gardens with friendly staff. Cool beachfront and garden suites, spa, swimming pool and whirlpool. The beach is lovely but not secluded, close to the centre of

Castries and alongside George F.L. Charles Airport. **$$$–$$$$**

There are three Sandals (www.sandals.com) all-inclusive, couples-only resorts on the island: **Sandals Halcyon Beach St Lucia**, Choc Bay, tel: 453 0222, **Sandals Regency St Lucia Golf Resort & Spa**, La Toc Road, tel: 452 3081 and **Sandals Grande St Lucian Spa & Beach Resort**, Pigeon Island Causeway, Gros Islet, tel: 455 2000. Guests may use the facilities of all three. **$$$$**

NORTH OF CASTRIES

Almond Morgan Bay, Gros Islet, tel: 450 2511; www.almondresorts.com. Large, luxury all-inclusive property on Choc with swimming pools, hot tub, water sports facilities and a volcanic sand beach. The spacious bedrooms are tastefully decorated and guests have a choice of a sea or garden view. Spa facilities and wedding packages are available. Children are welcome at this family-friendly resort. **$$$–$$$$**

Calabash Cove, Bonaire Estate, Marisule, tel: 456 3500; www.calabash cove.com. Quiet, delightful hotel of 26 rooms on hillside, beachfront property. Beach cottages on the water are large, wood-panelled suites with vine-covered deck, plunge pool, outdoor shower, hammocks and every luxury. Rooms in the main building are smaller but equally well-appointed. Excellent food, all-inclusive packages available but not mandatory, impeccable service and lush gardens. **$$$$**

East Winds Inn, Labrelotte Bay, tel: 452 8212; www.eastwinds.com. Small intimate, all-inclusive beachfront hotel with views of Labrelotte Bay and stylish cottage accommodation with 30 pretty rooms. The long-established hotel is set in lovely, lush tropical gardens and has a gourmet restaurant and piano bar. **$$$$**

Villa Beach Cottages, Choc Bay, tel: 450 2884; www.villabeachcottages.com. A collection of 20 self-contained cottages and suites situated on Choc Bay. Spacious rooms with air-conditioning, some with four poster beds, all with kitchens. Water sports facilities and pool. **$$$**

Windjammer Landing Resort, Labrelotte Bay, tel: 456 9000; www.windjammer-landing.com. Large, white timeshare property on a steep hillside with views over the bay. The resort has very comfortable accommodation in studios, apartments and villas, room only or with meal plans. Families welcome. Tennis, water sports, swimming pools and spa facilities. **$$$–$$$$**

RODNEY BAY

Bay Gardens Resorts, Rodney Bay, tel: 457 8006; www.baygardensresorts.com. There are three hotels in this locally owned group, all in Rodney Bay and popular with business and leisure travellers alike. The newest and most luxurious is the **Bay Gardens Beach Resort**, an all-suite hotel right on Reduit Beach with spa, fitness centre, car hire, dive shop and watersports. **Bay Gardens Hotel** and the smaller **Bay Gardens Inn** are in the heart of the village close to the road to Gros Islet. They have comfortable rooms and a high rate of repeat visitors, reflecting their popularity. **$$–$$$**

Caribbean Jewel Beach Resort, Gros Islet, tel: 452 9199; www.caribbean jewelresort.com. Spacious rooms and suites in a hillside property with magnificent views over Rodney Bay and out to Pigeon Island National Landmark. A good walk to village and beach. All accommodation has air-conditioning; the suites have balconies. Local restaurant on site. **$$**

Coco Palm, Rodney Bay Boulevard, tel: 456 2800; www.coco-resorts.com. Stylish mid-sized hotel in the village, a great location convenient for beach, nightlife and shopping, but set back from the road to eliminate noise. Comfortable rooms and suites overlook the pool or garden, the best being on the ground floor with French doors giving direct access to a patio and the pool. All well-equipped, with air-conditioning and Wi-Fi throughout. **$$–$$$**

Ginger Lily, Gros Islet, tel: 458 0300; www.thegingerlilyhotel.com. Small hotel across the road from Reduit Beach. Quiet and romantic, with simple spacious rooms, small pool and lovely gardens, with bars and restaurants within walking distance. **$$–$$$**

Harmony Suites, Rodney Bay, tel: 452 8756; www.harmonysuites.com. Comfortable, moderately priced suite accommodation near Reduit Beach with views of the marina; no children under 12 allowed. Acclaimed restaurant *The Edge* on site on the waterfront, with its sushi bar. **$$–$$$**

Rex Resorts, Reduit Beach, Rodney Bay, tel: 452 9999/8351; www.rexresorts. com. Two adjacent hotels **Royal** and **St Lucian**, on a prime part of the beach, offering a variety of rooms and suites with pool, garden or sea views and a range of meal plans, activities and sports. Have floodlit tennis courts. Plenty of eating options including the very good *Chic* gourmet restaurant and the *Oriental*, specialising in Far Eastern cuisine. **$$$–$$$$**

By the pool at LeSport (p.116)

NORTH COAST

Cap Maison, Smuggler's Cove Drive, Cap Estate, tel: 457 8670; www.capmaison. com. Luxury rooms, suites and villa suites with full kitchens in boutique hotel overlooking Smuggler's Cove. Spacious, comfortable, good facilities and attentive service. Panoramic views to Pigeon Point from the much-praised *Cliff at Cap* clifftop gourmet restaurant offering breakfast, lunch and dinner. Beach bar for daytime snacks, beach towels and water sports. **$$$–$$$$**

Cotton Bay Village, Cas-en-Bas, tel: 456 5700; www.cottonbaystlucia.com. A compact development on the Atlantic coast but protected from the ocean by rocks and a reef, so safe for swimming. Suites, townhouses and villas consisting of one to four bedrooms, many with their own private pools, while the most expensive have the luxury of 24-hour butler service. The resort is within walking distance of the golf course but remote from other amenities. **$$$–$$$$**

La Panache, Cas-en-Bas Road, Gros Islet, tel: 450 0765; www.saintlucianplants. com/lapanache. A small guest house with three simple, air-conditioned, self-catering apartments on a hillside with views from the balconies over Rodney Bay and Pigeon Island. Clean, friendly, relaxed and quiet, with lovely garden planted by a botanist. **$**

LeSport, Cariblue Beach, tel: 457 7800/450 8551; www.thebodyholiday.com. A luxury all-inclusive spa resort in the far north of the island set on a hillside with a palm-shaded beach; suites are spacious and tastefully furnished for couples or singles. Lots of activities and sports, from archery to yoga. The restaurants serve great food and there is live entertainment. Some spa treatments are included in the price. **$$$$**

Ocean View, Massade, Gros Islet, tel: 450 0833; www.oceanviewstlucia.com. A small hotel situated in the hills north of Rodney Bay. The comfortable rooms each have a balcony and a sea or garden view. Rooftop swimming pool and restaurant. Good value packages available. Children welcome. **$–$$**

Smugglers Cove Resort & Spa, Cap Estate, Anse Bécune, tel: 450 0551; www.smugglersresort.com. All-inclusive resort on 18 hectares (45 acres) of beautifully manicured gardens behind a lovely horseshoe-shaped cove with golden sand. Wheelchair-friendly, there are several categories of single storey rooms in village clusters, a variety of restaurants, several bars and swimming pools and spa. Popular with couples or families, there is a great kids' club and nursery as well as lots of activities from tai chi and yoga to squash, tennis and watersports. **$$$–$$$$**

MARIGOT BAY

Discovery at Marigot Bay, Marigot Bay, tel: 458 5300; www.marigotbay.com. Luxury resort on the hillside running down to the waterfront, lovely views of the harbour and the yachts, with every amenity. Gourmet restaurants and boutique shops at The Marina Village, as well as water sports at the marina. **$$$–$$$$**

Smugglers Cove Resort & Spa

The Inn On The Bay, Marigot Bay, tel: 451 4260; www.saint-lucia.com. A small adult-only bed & breakfast inn on the hilltop with a glorious view over the bay. Simple but comfortable rooms have fans and verandas which catch the breezes. Free shuttle to the bay area. $$–$$$

JJ's Paradise Resort, Marigot Bay, tel: 451 4076; www.jj-paradise.com. A St Lucian-owned and operated resort on a hillside, popular with the sailing fraternity because of its location close to sheltered Marigot Bay. Clean, spacious air-conditioned rooms, cottages and bungalows with teak furniture and verandas overlooking the bay. Breakfast available, restaurants nearby. $–$$

Marigot Beach Club Hotel & Dive Resort, Marigot Bay, tel: 451 4974; www.marigotdiveresort.com. Rooms and villas on the waterfront with great views of Marigot Bay out to the Caribbean Sea and also of the countryside. A popular place to stay for dive and water sports enthusiasts. It is also the home of the famous Doolittle's Restaurant. $$–$$$

Ti Kaye Village Resort, Anse Cochon, tel: 456 8101/2; www.tikaye.com. West coast hideaway on a cliffside south of Anse la Raye. Accommodation in stylish, romantic Caribbean-style cottages with outdoor showers in lush gardens. The beach is a short walk down and a long walk up 169 steps. Popular with honeymooners and a good choice for divers; the *Lesleen M* shipwreck is just offshore. Balinese staff man the clifftop spa overlooking the water, which uses only locally made, natural products. $$–$$$

SOUFRIÈRE

Anse Chastanet and Jade Mountain, Soufrière, tel: 459 7000; www.ansechastanet.com, www.jademountainstlucia.com. Lovely and spacious, open-sided but

> **Divers' Paradise**
> The warm, clear Caribbean waters that lap the island of St Lucia have made it popular with scuba divers and snorkellers. Several hotels and resorts offer dive holiday packages, which should cover all dive expenses and a stay in a comfortable hotel. Anse Chastanet, Ti Kaye, Windjammer Landing, The Inn On The Bay, Oasis Marigot and Almond Morgan Bay have comprehensive packages for divers and other water lovers.
>
> For more information contact the St Lucia Tourist Board in your home country or visit www.stlucia.org

private accommodation set on a hillside with breathtaking views of the Pitons, sea and forest. Stylish decoration and furnishings made from local wood and textiles. The Jade Mountain suites on the hilltop are modern, fabulously luxurious, romantic and breezy, each with its own infinity pool. Excellent restaurants and a lovely spa for pampering, with Scuba St Lucia and Bike St Lucia on site. Tennis, yoga, kayaking and other watersports available. The resort has a volcanic sand beach, but nearby Anse Mamin has a stretch of fine white sand. $$$–$$$$

Crystals, Soufrière, tel: 384 8995; www.stluciacrystals.com. Five rustic, quirky cottages with colourful décor and homely feel are a mixture of North African and plantation house style, with artwork scattered in every corner. Rooms all have a view of the Pitons. Each cottage has a full kitchen, air conditioning, plunge pool, swimming pool or Jacuzzi. The Tree House bar and restaurant is available for guests only, picnic lunches are available and help with excursions offered. Romantic and popular for weddings. $$$

Fond Doux Estate, Soufrière, tel: 459 7545; www.fonddouxestate.com. Pretty, traditional chattel houses have been moved from Castries and remodelled as comfortable guest accommodation on this working cocoa plantation. Peaceful countryside location set in tropical gardens around a French colonial estate house. **$$–$$$**

Hotel Chocolat, Rabot Estate, Soufrière, tel: UK: +44 (0)844 544 1272, US: +1-800-757-7132; www.the hotelchocolat.com. New in 2011, this is a boutique hotel of traditional-style wooden cottages and villas on a working cocoa estate with views of the Pitons. Clean lines with white linen and every luxury and comfort. Pleasant walks on the estate through fruit trees to historic battle sites, tours of the cocoa plantation and the chocolate making process. A spa will offer massages using local cocoa nibs, oil and butter. **$$$$**

Hummingbird Beach Resort, off the Anse Chastanet Road, tel: 459 7985; www.istlucia.co.uk. Small hotel on the west coast just outside Soufrière centre. Most rooms have a view of the sea and the Pitons as well as easy access to the beach. Cottage with kitchen also available. Restaurant on site. **$–$$$**

Jalousie Plantation (to be renamed The Tides Sugar Beach) Val des Pitons, Jalousie Bay, tel: 456 8000; www.thejalousieplantation.com. Luxury resort on lush former plantation extending back from a sheltered bay between the Pitons. Owned by Roger Myers, former accountant to the Rolling Stones, whose eclectic modern art collection is displayed around the hotel. The property has been extensively upgraded and expanded to be relaunched in 2011 with a new name. Villas are in tasteful clusters each with a butler, every comfort and absolute privacy. As well as tennis, a PADI dive centre and children's activities, the rainforest spa has treehouse gazebos built among the ruins of the old sugar plantation. Delicious food is offered in the restaurants while the ultra-modern, pop-art Cane Bar stocks specialty rums. **$$$$**

La Dauphine Estate, Soufrière, tel: 450 2884; www.villabeachcottages.com. Cottage and Great House for rent on a 19th-century plantation 8km (5 miles) from Soufrière. Rooms are decorated and furnished in colonial style and there are nature trails and forest close by where guests can hike. **$$**

La Haut Plantation, West Coast Road, Soufrière, tel: 459 7008; www.la haut.com. A family-run guesthouse with simple rooms, en suite bathrooms and private balcony. The best thing is the view of the Pitons, at half the price of the luxury hotels nearby. Not on the beach. A self-contained cottage is also available to rent. **$$–$$$**

Ladera Resort, Soufrière, tel: 459 7323; www.ladera.com. Upscale and exclusive hillside property of villas and suites 3km (2 miles) from the centre of Soufrière. Accommodation, crafted from stone and rich hardwood, is open on one side, has beautiful furnishings and private plunge pool. Lovely tropical gardens and breathtaking views over Soufrière Bay to the Pitons; excellent cuisine at the award-winning *Dasheene Restaurant*. Spa treatments and warm mineral pools for bathing. **$$$–$$$$**

Mago Estate Hotel, West Coast Road, tel: 459 5880; www.magohotel.com. In the hills just above Soufrière, overlooking the Pitons. Accommodation is scattered throughout lush gardens with tropical fruit trees and hammocks. Rooms have an open side from which to view Soufrière Bay. En suite facilities. Plunge pool and a swimming pool. New Carib suites have kitchenettes. **$$$–$$$$**

Stonefield Estate Villa Resort, Soufrière, tel: 459 7037; www.stonefield villas.com. Small villa complex in beautifully landscaped gardens almost 2km (1 mile) from Soufrière. Each villa has 1–3 bedrooms and is individual; some have a garden shower, a veranda and panoramic views of the Pitons, the sea and Soufrière. Swimming pool and a good restaurant on site as well as a spa which uses local products including chocolate wraps using home-grown cocoa. $$$–$$$$

VIEUX FORT AND THE SOUTH

Balenbouche Estate, tel: 455 1244; www.balenbouche.com. Family-run guest-house with colonial-style villas to rent on an 18th-century sugar plantation that remains a working organic farm. A popular heritage site *(see page 77)* with tropical gardens, containing huge old trees and machinery from the sugar mill including an old water wheel, it is used for weddings and yoga retreats. Amerindian artifacts have been discovered on the 30-hectare (75-acre) property. Friendly, intimate, with a rustic, faded glory feel. Delicious home-cooked food available. $–$$

Mirage Beach, Laborie, tel: 455 9237; www.cavip.com/mirage. Right on the beach, this small, rustic hotel is set in beautiful tropical gardens in a fishing community. Quiet and away from the tourist hustle, there's a 2-bedroom apartment upstairs and master bedroom downstairs, both with kitchenettes. There are good local restaurants in the village or meals can be prepared for you in your apartment by local cooks. $–$$

The Reef, Anse de Sables, tel: 454 3418, www.slucia.com/reef. A few rustic wooden huts tucked behind the popular café on the beach. Ideal for windsurfers and kitesurfers who don't mind basic lodgings – there is no hot water but it's heated by the sun. Fans and mosquito nets are provided and breakfast on the beach is included. $

EAST COAST

Fox Grove Inn, Mon Repos, Micoud, tel: 455 3271; www.foxgroveinn.com. Small country hotel close to Mamiku Gardens. The 12 simple guestrooms and self-contained apartments have en suite showers or bathrooms and ceiling fans. Surrounded by banana and coconut plantations with good views of Praslin Bay. Popular with nature-lovers. Good restaurant on site. $

The 19th-century colonial Great House at the Balenbouche Estate

INDEX